Teaching Effective Classroom Routines

Joe Witt   Lynn LaFleur   Gale Naquin   Donna Gilbertson

Teaching Effective Classroom Routines

05   04   03   02   6   5   4   3

ISBN 1-57035-162-7

Edited by Francelia Sevin and Beverly Rokes
Text layout and design by Tracy Katzenberger
Cover design by Tracy Katzenberger
Cover image © 1993 by Tom McCarthy Photos
Photography by Lynn LaFleur

Printed in the United States of America

Published and distributed by

SOPRIS
WEST

4093 Specialty Place • Longmont, CO 80504 • (303) 651-2829 • www.sopriswest.com

114TEACH/5-02/C&M/1.5M/602

To all teachers everywhere who are
determined to create the best
environment for all children

Acknowledgments

We acknowledge gratefully the support of the following people:

Phyllis Crawford, Principal, who offered her school as a place for the advancement of education. Thank you for your enthusiasm and direction, Phyllis!

The essential conditions of teaching must be choice, passion, a desire for knowledge, and good skills. The teachers at Audubon Elementary School teach under these conditions. Their careful, deliberate teachings have helped shape the academic and social behaviors of many children.

Special thanks to Renee Baily, Monica Bergeron, Dawn Brumfield, Judy Burch, Stacy Clegg, Cleland Strickland, Heather Gaspard, Andrea Harris, Caprice Hayes, Jeanette Moore, Caroline Lee, Nora Miller, Scott Moore, Christine Santhin, Toni Teeple, Julie Wright, and Beth Yglesias, who supported our efforts in researching and provided expertise, support, and their invaluable talents as teachers.

Thanks also to the teachers in East Baton Rouge Parish, La., who offered thoughtful suggestions and made it possible for this work to be expanded and be seen by teachers everywhere. The teachers in this parish have provided living proof that the routines presented in this book *can* be done!

About the Authors

Joseph C. Witt, Ph.D.

Throughout his professional career, Joe Witt has been actively pursuing answers to questions about how professionals in schools can work together to prevent and remediate problems. This pursuit has led him to publish over 100 papers and 12 books. The source of his writing for the past 10 years has been his work with the LSU Behavior Intervention Team, which provides direct service to schools and children in Louisiana. Through the collaboration with teachers and other professionals, he has worked to develop strategies that have face validity, are practical for use in classrooms, and are connected to the effective schools literature. In turn, this work has been acknowledged externally. Dr. Witt has, for example, received recognition in the form of being named an honorary lifetime member of the Louisiana School Psychologists Association, Editor of *School Psychology Quarterly*, LSU Alumni Distinguished Professor, Lightner Witmer Award (APA, Div 16), APA Fellow, Editor of *Guilford School Practitioner Series*, and Associate Editor of the *Buros Mental Measurements Yearbook* and *School Psychology Review*. Dr. Witt has also received over 20 externally funded grants and research contracts.

Lynn Habyan LaFleur, Ph.D.

Dr. LaFleur holds a master's degree in educational administration and school psychology and a doctorate in psychology. She is presently a behavior consultant in East Baton Rouge, Louisiana, where she provides inservices for schools, teacher training and coaching in effective teaching strategies, and assessments and behavioral treatments for students referred for behavior and academic problems. Dr. LaFleur also serves as a coordinator for the elementary alternative education program, Academy for Diverse Learners, which is a preventative program in Baton Rouge for students experiencing difficulties in their regular education setting. Her interests include school-based consultation, effective teaching behaviors such as class and schoolwide management, generalization and maintenance of behavior, and assessment and treatment of children with behavior and academic difficulties.

Gale Mayronne Naquin, Ph.D.

Gale Naquin is currently the project director of the Prereferral Assessment Model (PAM) at the University of New Orleans. Throughout her professional career she has been actively involved in developing ways to bring research into practice. She has more than 27 years of educational experience as a classroom teacher, an administrator at the state and local levels in both the public and private education sector, an educational diagnostician, and a university professor.

For years she has served as a leader in the Council for Exceptional Children. She is a past president of The Council of Educational Diagnostic Services (CEDS) and the Louisiana Federation of CEC. She is currently an officer in the Louisiana Teacher Education Division of CEC.

Gale has been a friend of Sopris West for many years. She is a trainer for several Sopris products, including *Basic Skill Builders*, *Systematic Screening for Behavior Disorders*, and *Project RIDE*. She is presently working with colleagues and Sopris in preparing new teacher institutes and summer trainings. Her research interests and expertise include assessment techniques, teacher efficacy, organizational reform of the referral process, and service delivery for students at risk. Gale has presented over 200 papers at national and local conferences. She has served as consultant for public and private school districts, advocacy groups, and mental health providers.

Donna Gilbertson, Ph.D.

Donna Gilbertson is an assistant professor of psychology at Utah State University. Her professional activities include helping adults respond effectively to children's learning and behavioral adjustment problems in school settings through research activities, teacher training, and consultation services in public schools. Currently, she is examining the use of informal assessment strategies with bilingual students to better link educators with effective instructional strategies. She is also modifying a systematic screening model that considers language proficiency, functional assessment, and intervention responsiveness for decreasing over-representation of minorities in special education. Finally, she continues to investigate consultation strategies to help teachers and parents use effective strategies such as routines that are designed to help children in their care.

Contents

Introduction

When students are asked what they need to do to be successful in school, many reply with "don'ts": "Don't hit, don't curse, don't spit," etc. Students usually know what not to do but often don't know what to do. It might seem like children should "just know" how to complete simple classroom tasks, such as putting materials away and quietly returning to their desks. The seasoned teacher knows better: Some students naturally learn basic school skills while others have difficulties like dawdling and touching students on the way back to their seats.

Teaching students how to perform basic school skills prevents behavior problems and saves precious instructional time. Research shows that effective and ineffective teachers respond to misbehaviors in the same ways. For example, when a student fails to work quietly at his or her desk, most teachers will prompt the student to begin working. The chief difference between effective and ineffective teachers is that effective teachers do much more to prevent problems. An effective teacher will teach students how to work quietly, give specific steps on how to do the work, and provide a time limit before asking students to do the work. By actively teaching students how to do a classroom routine, the teacher guides them to perform the routine accurately. The teacher also provides feedback on how the students are performing. Once the students learn what to do and when to do it, the teacher can easily signal them to begin a routine and monitor them as they do that routine.

If students are able to do routines quickly, they will get to work in a timely manner. Further, when students are taught to be responsible for certain jobs, such as grading their own papers, monitoring homework notebooks, and signing out for a bathroom break, even more teaching time is saved. As a result, teachers can spend more time on instructional activities and are able to provide students with more academic learning opportunities during the school day.

How do classroom routines prevent problems? When children know what they are supposed to do, they are less likely to do what they are not supposed to do. Generally, children like structure and respond positively to it. We have observed many classrooms in which the time taken to transition from one subject to another was greater than 8 minutes. We have also observed classrooms in which that same transition was accomplished in under 30 seconds! Now, if it takes only 30 seconds to actually make the transition, what do you think students are doing during the rest of the time when they take 8 minutes or more to transition to their next subject? Some students will wait patiently but others will find ways to fill their time. By teaching a transitioning routine, the teacher will be in control of what the children do, not the children.

Effective teachers systematically teach basic classroom routines and procedures. In terms of transition times alone, research has shown that teachers can save more than an hour of instructional time per day by systematically teaching students how to properly negotiate the 8-15 transitions of a typical school day (LaFleur, Witt, Naquin, Harwell, & Gilbertson, 1998). Research also supports training students in other routines (Berlinger, 1989; Evertson et al., 1986; Gettinger, 1988). Classrooms with specific procedures for getting assistance, turning in work, working independently or in groups, and lining up have fewer off-task and disruptive behaviors than classrooms without such procedures (Emmer & Evertson, 1981). Teachers who develop and use classroom routines need to spend little time getting organized and dealing with misconduct. Consequently, their classrooms attain high task-engagement rates, which is powerfully correlated with student achievement (Brophy, 1986). The routines described in this book are those that have been identified by teachers, principals, and other educators as the ones most commonly needed during the school day.

What is Behavior Class? Most teachers include a reading class, a math class, and so forth, in their curriculum, in which they teach children math, reading, and other skills. Few teachers, however, include a formal class to teach the behaviors they expect students to use in the classroom. We call this type of class Behavior Class. Behavior Class lasts perhaps 5-10 minutes a day during the first 6 weeks of the school year, when the behaviors are being systematically taught. The class time can then be reduced to 3-5 minutes. Teachers can use this book as a starting point for the curriculum. Every few days a new skill (such as how to ask for teacher assistance) can be taught and practiced. Through the use of a separate Behavior Class, teachers can ensure that important skills are actually taught.

A Behavior Class, then, is a 3-10 minute period set aside each day to introduce or review a specific classroom routine. During the class, students are taught the routines step-by-step and then practice the routines until they have them down pat. Behavior Classes, similar to reading and math classes, ensure that all students know what they should do. When students know the behaviors expected of them, they have no excuse for noncompliance. Behavior Classes also hold students accountable when they do not follow the rules as instructed. A logical consequence for not following the rules is requiring practice during times that are inconvenient for the student (e.g., during recess).

We recommend that Behavior Classes be scheduled during regular class time. We feel this is reasonable, because teaching expected behaviors will save class time in the long run. However, if students do not use the skills they have been taught, we recommend that additional practice occur during students' free time. If students use up content time with play, we feel their play time should be used for review and practice of the behaviors they should be using. Not only will this review and practice reinforce skill use, but it will also help students connect problem behaviors with consequences.

The ultimate goal is to have the basic school skills become routine. Compliance should be automatic and unnoticed by students and teachers alike. When implemented correctly, Behavior Class eliminates repeated requests and reminders to perform tasks in certain ways. Rather than spending time explaining how to hand in papers or line up correctly, teachers can spend that time teaching, being creative, and helping students learn—not scolding, nagging, or punishing.

Three Reasons to Implement Behavior Classes

1. **Save Instructional Time.** While Behavior Classes take up some instructional time at the beginning of the year, they save instructional time in the long run.

2. **Prevent Behavior Problems.** By showing students what is expected of them and providing structure to the classroom environment, Behavior Classes help to avert many problem behaviors.

3. **Free Teachers From Correcting Misbehaviors.** When students automatically pass in papers, clean up after themselves, and perform other routine functions, teachers are freed to do other things, such as administrative duties and review of student work.

A major part of this book discusses classroom routines. By routines, we are referring to activities that occur daily or even many times daily, such as handing in papers, asking for assistance, and transitioning from one activity to another. In addition to providing a step-by-step guide for teaching the basic routines, this book provides the following complementary materials. First, Overhead Transparency Masters are provided that list the behaviors the students need to learn for each routine. Second, Classroom Checklists are included. The checklists outline, sequentially, the behaviors that both the teacher and the students need to do during each routine. You can use the checklists to obtain feedback on your teaching of a routine by having a colleague observe you in action and check off the steps you complete. Since the steps are organized sequentially, it is easy for someone to follow along and note whether Step 1, Step 2, etc., was completed. The Checklists can also be used in conjunction with a bug-in-the-ear device to facilitate the learning of a routine. A bug-in-the-ear device is a relatively inexpensive walkie-talkie-like transmitter that allows a "coach" to observe a teacher implementing a routine and to prompt the teacher if a step is missed by talking quietly as the teacher listens through a small earphone (i.e., bug). Teachers can thus be "silently" reminded of each step without students being aware that cues are being given. These devices sell for less than $100.00 at retail outlets.

Finally, "Classroom Coaches" are available from the publisher as a supplement to this book. These small cards summarize each step of the routines to provide you with a quick cue as you teach the routines. They can also be used as reminders when practicing the routine with your students. The advantage of the Classroom Coaches is that they provide a quick reference that you can carry with you as you are helping the class to practice a particular skill.

Although this book covers the most commonly needed classroom routines in the view of the teachers, principals, and other educators we surveyed, individual teachers will have specific expectations not covered here. You are encouraged to create your own lesson plans to teach such skills to your class.

Remember: The goal is to teach students how to perform basic school skills. The key to conducting a productive classroom is to show students step-by-step what to do; let them practice the routine a few times; and have them practice more if they fail to follow the steps correctly.

The routines in this book are designed primarily for elementary aged children, but similar routines can and have been used with children (and adults!) of all ages. The procedures are ideal for both general and special education teachers.

Materials Required

All of the materials required to teach a Behavior Class, with the exception of a kitchen timer, are included in this book. As noted earlier, we have provided dark masters listing the student steps for each routine that can easily be photocopied onto overhead transparencies, so it is helpful to have access to transparencies and an overhead projector. However, the steps can also be listed on the blackboard or a flip chart for easy viewing by the class. Finally, as was also noted earlier, you may want to acquire a bug-in-the-ear transmitter that you can use with the assistance of a colleague or the principal to provide quiet reminders of important steps in the routines.

Preparation

Imagine a typical school day and think about what you expect students to do as the day progresses. What are the common situations encountered? For example, do you expect students to raise their hands and wait patiently for assistance? Write down every expected behavior you can think of. Then skim through the Contents page of this book and add the relevant routines to your list. You may also want to ask teachers you respect about the routines they find most important during the school day.

Next, prioritize your list based on the behaviors you feel need to be taught first. Generally, they are the behaviors used most frequently. For example, after reviewing the routines that are presented in this book, you may decide that you need to first teach students how to start the school day in an efficient and productive manner by using the "Beginning the School Day" routine. Next in importance may be to teach students how to get your help ("Requesting Assistance" routine), how to do their work independently ("Independent Practice" routine), how to grade their work ("Student Grading" routine), and how to turn in the work to you ("Passing In Papers" routine).

Once you have finished prioritizing your list, determine which of the routines are covered in this book. For any that are not covered in this book, you will need to create your own. To do so, you simply follow the format of the routines provided here, making adjustments to fit your particular needs.

Remember, as you create your list of routines, that students like structure. It reduces their uncertainty. Most students also want to do the right thing. Once they are shown the correct behaviors, they are usually glad to use them. Clear guidelines also result in students' expecting other students to do things the right way.

Organization of the Book

The routines in this book are organized into five sections: teacher routines, basic student routines, responsible student routines, transition routines, and special behavior routines. Each routine begins with a rationale for using the routine, which is followed by the goals that will be met when the routine is implemented. Next, the steps the teacher needs to do in preparation for teaching the routine are described. And finally, the teacher is led, step-by-step, through the procedure of training students to use the routine.

The "Teacher Routines" section covers important teacher behaviors that you can use to get your students to behave on a daily basis. For example, the "Signaling for Attention" routine provides an effective strategy that immediately gets students to notice when you want them to stop, look, and listen. Following the teacher routines are routines that teach students how to behave as you expect them to in the classroom. Students are first taught basic routines, including procedures for getting their materials organized and for requesting teacher assistance. Next, students are taught routines for carrying out responsible tasks, such as working independently or grading their work. The transition routines teach students how to quickly prepare for new activities. Finally, a few special-behavior routines are presented, such as routines for welcoming visitors.

Following the teacher and student routines is a section of reproducibles—forms and letters described in the routines that you can photocopy for use in your classroom. Next is the section of Classroom Checklists, the worksheets provided as a means of helping teachers receive feedback on their teaching of the routines. A colleague or administrator observing you teach a routine can easily put a check on the worksheet next to the steps that you complete accurately and an X next to the steps that you miss or complete inaccurately, giving you a good indication of what you need to do differently the next time you teach the routine.

The Overhead Transparency Masters make up the next section of the book. These outlines of the steps the students need to do to accurately perform an expected behavior are useful teaching aids. Before you teach a routine, we recommend that you pull out the relevant transparency and review the student steps that will need to be taught, demonstrated, and practiced. Then, during a training session, place the transparency on an overhead projector for students to view. The students can read the steps as you explain and model the routine and refer to the steps when first attempting to perform the routine. Finally, the transparencies contain a chart that you can use to provide feedback to the students on their performance during training sessions. By using the chart to record the steps the students completed accurately during a trial run of a routine as well as the steps they missed or performed inaccurately, you can give students a good idea of their progress.

The final teaching aids provided are the Classroom Coaches, which are available from the publisher as a supplement to this book. You can carry these small cards, which contain outlines of the steps teachers are to implement when using a routine, with you for easy reference when you are actively using the routines.

We recommend that this book be used as a starting point for teaching effective classroom behaviors. It contains the most commonly needed routines and breaks them down into simple steps, each of which is a behavior. The curriculum needed to teach each routine is clearly laid out in a tell, show, and do format. This means that in teaching a skill, the first step is to tell the children the expected behaviors. The next step is to show the children the behavior by modeling it yourself or having other students demonstrate it. The last step is to have each student practice the behavior while you provide feedback.

The "tell" phase is facilitated by the overhead transparencies. The Classroom Coaches can help you with the "do" phase, since they provide a convenient reminder of each step. Finally, how well you carry out all three steps will be facilitated by use of the Classroom Checklists, since the feedback you receive will help you improve your teaching in each area of the tell, show, and do format.

We referred to this book as a starting point, since we realize that every classroom is different and every teacher manages the classroom a little bit differently. Hence, most teachers will want to create their own routines in addition to the ones listed here or to modify the steps we've laid out. Because each routine has been broken down into simple steps, a little twist here and there is likely all that will be needed.

Does It Work?

The techniques described in this book are consistent with validated practices found in the effective schools and effective teaching literature. We mentioned earlier that research has shown that effective and ineffective teachers respond to inappropriate behavior in the same way but that effective teachers do more to prevent behavior problems from occurring. In particular, they engage in many "beginning of the year" activities, especially teaching children classroom routines and expected behaviors, which, in the long run, save classroom time and prevent behavior problems (Emmer, Evertson, & Anderson, 1980; Gettinger, 1988). For example, research on transitions in the classroom has concluded the following:

- Spending time teaching cues, determining schedules and activities, and providing feedback early in the school year reduces problems that may occur due to transitioning (Emmer & Evertson, 1981).

- Successful transitioning involves: (1) teachers being prepared, so that transition time is just for putting away materials for one subject and taking out those for another, and (2) students being taught appropriate transitioning behaviors that are practiced until demonstrated (Jenson, Sloane, & Young, 1988).

- Transition time can be cut by over 50% when teachers systematically train students to transition (LaFleur, Witt, Naquin, Harwell, & Gilbertson, 1998).

Additional evidence on the effectiveness of teaching students expected behaviors has been provided by Emmer and Evertson (1981). Among other things, they found that effective teachers monitor students by walking around the classroom, scan for student compliance to directions, and check students' work. In elementary grades, the monitoring of behavior has been shown to be highly correlated with academic achievement (Rosenshine & Stevens, 1986). Other factors that have been correlated with academic achievement include having in place clear student procedures for how students can get help, for what students should do when they are finished with their work, and for how students can get immediate feedback on their completed work.

What If It Doesn't Work?

The classroom routines in this book are designed for all students, including those who require individualized behavior programs. The task of assisting students with more serious behavior problems is made easier by having well-established routines and clear behavioral expectations. For more serious behavioral concerns, you are referred to *The Teacher's Encyclopedia of Behavior Management* (Sprick & Howard, 1995) and *The Tough Kid Book* (Rhode, Jenson, & Reavis, 1993).

Scheduling

Behavior Classes are most effective when they are routine, systematic, and ongoing, just like any other basic skills class. In addition, the effective teaching literature strongly supports building good behavioral habits early in the school year. In fact, the literature recommends that teachers make a concerted effort during the first 6 weeks of the school year to teach common classroom routines. After the skills are in place, they become automatic and require less systematic teaching. Although initiating Behavior Classes at the beginning of the year is ideal, they will be effective whenever they are initiated.

In addition to being taught early in the school year, skills should be taught regularly. A time should be scheduled each day for Behavior Class, just as for

Sample School Day Schedule

Reading Class	8:00–8:45
Behavior Class	8:45–8:55
(may require a little more time at the beginning of the year and less time as the year progresses)	
Recess	9:00–9:25
Math	9:30–10:15
Journal	10:15–11:00
Lunch	11:00–11:40
Language Arts	11:45–12:30
Art	12:30–1:30
Social Studies	1:30–2:30

> "Clearly, the beginning of the year is a critical time for establishing behavior patterns, expectations, and procedures that can persist throughout the year."
>
> Everston & Emmer, 1981

core subjects. Some teachers incorporate Behavior Class into a morning class meeting. The advantage of this time slot is that it can be used extensively for Behavior Class early in the year and can be used for other class concerns as the year progresses.

Behavior Class Procedures

Material is taught in Behavior Class through a five-step process: (1) telling students the skill to be learned, (2) showing students how the skill should and should not be performed, (3) having students do the skill, (4) having students practice the skill, and (5) monitoring/reteaching the skill. The first three steps constitute the formal classroom lesson. In the practice phase, the skill is embedded within normal classroom routines. During the monitor/reteach phase, students are expected to perform the skill correctly when opportunities arise. If students don't use the skill, a reteaching routine provides additional practice.

Initial Instruction

When teaching a new skill in Behavior Class, use the same methods you use to teach reading or math skills. The time requirements for the initial classroom lesson will vary from skill to skill and class to class. Some teachers break the introductory lesson into separate sessions over a period of 2–3 days. The initial instruction includes the first three steps (tell, show, and do).

1. **Tell**

    Gain student attention and then introduce the topic, saying, for example, "Today's Behavior Class is about how to pass in completed papers and tests." A quick summary will tell the students what the skill involves: "Passing in papers includes putting your name and date on the paper and, at my cue, quietly and quickly handing it to the person on your right. Always place your paper at the top of the pile. The 'Paper Captain' will pick up the papers at the last desk of each row."

Providing a rationale for each new skill is also important. For the example just cited, you might say, "Passing in papers in this way will ensure that papers are handed in quietly and that we don't waste our learning time. It's also a way of allowing me to determine whose papers are whose should any be unsigned."

Conclude the "tell" phase by explaining each step in detail. Review each step of the procedure, and tell students exactly how to perform each step. It is often helpful to give the students a rationale for performing the steps in the desired ways. For example, papers are passed from side to side rather than back to front because there is less opportunity for students to hit or bother the people in front of them. Also in this phase, let students know if there is a time limit or goal to be met in the routine.

2. **Show**

In this phase, each step of the procedure is modeled. Show the class exactly how the skill is to be performed. Often it is helpful to have students assist with the demonstration. Include both positive and negative examples. Show students what to do and what not to do. Avoid gray areas, which are open to interpretation. Explain that there is a correct way to do the task and that there are incorrect ways to do the task. There is nothing in between.

3. **Do**

The "do" phase provides an opportunity for the entire class to perform the skill. Provide at least five opportunities for the class to perform the skill during the introductory lesson. Monitor student behavior closely, and provide feedback about correct and incorrect performance. As you watch, be sure to provide positive reinforcement. Make it a goal to say three to five positive comments for every negative or corrective comment. Directing your attention and that of the students toward those who are making improvement will help to *build* the skill.

Practice

When a new reading or math skill is introduced, students need to practice it with plenty of support and feedback. The learning of new behaviors is no different. Build a little extra time into the daily classroom schedule for practicing the new skill.

For example, when it comes time for students to use the newly learned skill of passing in papers, step the students through the process at a slow, deliberate pace. Give the class lots of reminders about how to perform the task correctly. Comment often about students who are using the new skill correctly. As students make fewer errors, three things begin to happen. First, the pace of the process picks up. The class will be able to accomplish the task in the allotted time. Second, you'll need to use fewer reminders and won't have to make as much of a conscious effort to teach the skill. The students will already know it. Third, fluency and automaticity increase. The skill will fade into the background and no one will have to think about the specific steps. This phase requires approximately 1 week but varies depending on the class.

Monitor and Reteach

Monitor

As new behaviors become automatic, your role will shift to monitoring. Make sure all students are using the skill every time it is required. If you allow one student to neglect to use a skill or to use it incorrectly, others may get the idea that they don't have to use the skill correctly either. Expecting all students to use the skill all of the time will prevent this from happening.

If your colleagues are also implementing Behavior Classes, take turns observing the students in one another's classes. Sometimes the process becomes so automatic that teachers become complacent and don't notice when some students are developing bad habits. A colleague who is there to monitor the process can help identify students who are performing the skill incorrectly.

Reteach

If one or more students fail to use a particular skill, those students or the entire class must spend time learning it again. Since the skill has already been taught and practiced, students have no excuse for not using it.

When students fail to demonstrate a skill, simply say, "It seems you have not learned how to _____, so we will need to practice this skill some more." Rather than using instructional time for practice, use a time such as recess, a free period, or after school. Have the students spend their recess passing in papers or walking back and forth to the lunchroom several times. By doing so, you will link the consequence directly to the problem. Most students will not want to spend their free time practicing a skill, so they will be motivated to perform future skills correctly on a regular basis.

Rather than requiring only those students who don't use a skill correctly to stay and practice it, some teachers require that the entire class take part in the practice session. The advantage of this method is that peer pressure will motivate students to perform skills correctly. The disadvantage is that it unfairly penalizes students who do what they are supposed to do.

Teacher Routines

Teaching is hard work. When you think about all of the administrative jobs teachers have to accomplish during the school day, it is a wonder any teaching gets done at all. But lessons are taught! And, in addition, students are greeted, book bags are put away, small-group activities are conducted, students line up for lunch, and pencils are sharpened. These are just a few of the activities that need to occur during any school day.

The teacher has two choices with regard to how classroom routines are accomplished. They can occur in a haphazard fashion, or they can occur in an orderly and deliberate manner. We know from research that a well-planned instructional approach to all classroom activities, including routines, can prevent the occurrence of behavior problems (Colvin, Sugai, Good, Young-Yon, & Lee, 1997; Gettinger, 1988; LaFleur et al., 1998). Such an approach includes the teaching of clearly defined and well-established routines, frequent monitoring of behavior, and social praise for compliance.

The purpose of this book is to help you streamline classroom routines and thereby increase instructional time. A routine is an activity that occurs regularly. For example, every day, students are going to come to school and enter the classroom, go to lunch, go to recess, take a bathroom break, and leave the classroom to go home. In between these activities, other routines occur, such as getting the teacher's attention, grading papers, and cleaning up. If teachers are to maximize instructional time, these routine activities cannot take up too much time. You cannot, however, assume that students will know how to conduct the everyday classroom routines in the manner you expect. Instead, you must deliberately teach the routines to your students just like you teach them math and reading. Students need to know what the routines are, what they look like when done right, and how to do them. And then, they need to be held accountable for their behavior.

Ideally, you should begin to carefully examine the routines that you want to occur in your classroom weeks before the school year starts. This book will give you a head start, since it details many of the basic routines in a recipe format. It is important to become familiar with the steps involved in each routine before you teach your students how to accomplish them. As you teach the routines, use the overhead transparencies included in this book to maintain group focus and provide a visual of the steps the students are expected to learn.

Side note: Teaching students to accomplish routine tasks quickly can be made more fun with a technique call Beat-the-Buzzer (Drabman & Creedon, 1979). This technique serves to reduce students' off-task behaviors during routines such as classroom transitions. The first step is to determine the amount of time that will be needed to complete the task. For example, you may decide that students should be able to put away their spelling work and take out their math textbook and workbook within 2 minutes. The second step is to tell the students how much time they have to complete the task and that you'll set a timer for that amount of time. Explain that the goal is for all students to complete the activity before the timer buzzes. Be sure to offer encouragement to the students during the activity. And finally, following the activity, be sure to apply appropriate consequences for beating or not beating the buzzer.

Greeting and Escorting Students To and From School

Rationale

Greeting students as they arrive at school will help to ensure order and safety as they make their way to the classroom. By monitoring bus and car pool arrival, as well as activities in the playground, bathrooms, and other out-of-classroom areas, teachers are able to prevent such problems as student wandering, which can lead to scuffles, fights, or destruction of property. Teaching students to arrive at the classroom in an orderly fashion includes preparing them through discussion, role-play, and the demonstration of appropriate behaviors as well as monitoring their behavior and providing feedback. Reminding students before they leave school about expected morning arrival behavior, and then following up in the morning, will help ensure that the day will start in a positive manner.

It is helpful to also have a routine for when students are departing the school. As in the morning, teachers and other school staff can position themselves at various places throughout the school. Staff stationed by the buses can both monitor students walking onto the buses and bid them a warm farewell.

Goals

To greet students as they get off the bus or are dropped off and remind them to walk to their assigned areas. To monitor students so that they walk in an orderly fashion without bothering other students. To provide feedback about arrival behavior by praising appropriate and correcting inappropriate actions.

Preparation

Assign staff members to:
- ☐ Greet cars
- ☐ Greet buses
- ☐ Monitor playgrounds
- ☐ Monitor the breakfast line
- ☐ Monitor the bathrooms
- ☐ Monitor the school gyms
- ☐ Monitor the halls
- ☐ Monitor other places

Create a Checklist to Make Sure All Areas Are Covered

1. Direct car and bus traffic to enter in one direction and leave in another in the same manner each morning.

2. Determine the areas that need to be supervised at your school. (Putting Xs on a map is helpful.)

3. Determine how many supervisors are needed for each area. Make sure that there are enough supervisors in each area to be able to see all of the students at all times.

4. Have students report to specific areas upon arrival at school each morning. Consider inclement weather when assigning areas, and make sure each is well supervised.

5. Assign teachers or other staff to supervise each area on specific days.

6. At the end of the day, students are dismissed over the school intercom (i.e., bus numbers are called, walkers and riders in car pools are dismissed), instruct teachers to stand by their doors so that they can monitor students in their classrooms as well as those walking in the halls.

7. As in the morning, supervisors should be assigned specific days to monitor areas throughout the school and in the bus and car zone.

Training

Refer to the "Arriving at School" Overhead.

1. Train teachers, bus drivers, and other staff supervisors to greet, monitor, and provide feedback to students as they arrive at school. Such training should be done before the first day of school.

2. Review the "Arriving at School" Overhead with them, so that everyone knows exactly what behavior is expected of the students.

3. Set aside classroom time on the first day of school to tell, show, and practice the procedures with your students. Train all students in arrival procedures by:

    *   Discussing the importance of safe bus behavior and passenger behavior in cars/vans

    *   Showing the students their assigned areas

    *   Telling, showing, and practicing with students how to wait for the "Car Greeter" or "Bus Greeter," walk off the bus or get out of the passenger side of the car, and walk to their assigned areas

    *   Reviewing the "Arriving at School" Overhead with the students

"Good morning to you, good morning to you. We're all in our places with nice smiling faces."

Refer to the "Departing From School" Overhead.

1. Train teachers, staff, and bus drivers to monitor the students' behavior.

2. Review the "Departing From School" Overhead with them, so that they know exactly what behavior is expected of the students.

3. Clearly instruct students to wait quietly in their seats and listen for their bus number to be announced over the school intercom.

4. Tell, show, and practice with students how to walk out of the classroom and to their bus or car pool line when they hear their bus number called or are dismissed to their car pools.

Greeting Students As They Arrive at School:

Students move quickly and safely onto school grounds.

① Greet

Students remain on the bus or in the car until the "Bus Greeter" or "Car Greeter" arrives at the bus door or gives the car pool signal and says:

"Good morning. Please walk quietly to your assigned area."

> Assigned areas may include specific areas of the playground or school (e.g., cafeteria, gym, classroom).

② Monitor

Watch students as they walk out of the bus single file to their assigned areas.

Optional:

Tally how many students do not know how to follow the steps. If a large number of students need practice, the routine may need to be retaught. Assign extra supervisors if necessary until the majority of students walk (and don't run) to their assigned areas.

③ Feedback

Praise students when they walk off the bus in single file. Say, for example:

"You really know how to wait your turn getting off the bus."

The principal can also provide praise during morning announcements.

or

Redirect/Correct. Say, for example:

"When you get off the bus, walk, don't run, down each step. Jumping is not correct. You could fall and get hurt. Wait here until everyone is off the bus and then practice going down the steps for me."

In such a case, have the student wait by your side until you are free to give him or her your full attention. Then watch the student practice getting off the bus and walking down the steps.

Escorting Students As They Depart From School:

Students move quickly and safely from school grounds.

① Announcements

Announce that the bus numbers and car pools will begin to be called out.

Remind students to walk quietly to their bus/cars when their bus number or car pool is called.

② Monitor

Stand at your classroom door to **monitor** students in your class and students walking in the hallway.

Make sure your students sit quietly at their desks listening for their bus number to be called.

Have staff watch students walking in the hallways and forming a straight line on the sidewalk in front of the bus door or in the car pool line.

Have staff make sure students walk onto the bus quietly and without touching anyone.

③ Feedback

Staff should **praise** students as they walk onto the bus in single file. They might say,

"Everyone has walked to their seats very patiently today."

Redirect/correct. Say, for example,

"You must walk up each step as you get on the bus without touching anyone. Pushing is not correct. Your friend could fall and get hurt. Go back to the end of the line and practice getting on the bus correctly."

Signaling for Attention

Rationale

Students who do not pay attention often need directions to be repeated or require redirection when tasks are done incorrectly, taking up valuable academic time. Setting up a system in which students immediately give you their full attention when you give a specific signal allows everyone to hear the directions you give.

Goal

To have students give you their full attention whenever you signal.

Preparation

Develop a signal that:

- Grabs your students' attention immediately

- Is easy and convenient to give

Teacher Signal Bank
- Clap several times
- Turn the lights off and then back on
- Call out, "Attention please!"
- Count to three
- Hold up your hand
- Ring a bell
- Make a timer go off
- Call out, "Freeze!"

Training

Refer to the "When the Teacher Signals" Overhead.

1. Tell the students that you have a signal you're going to use whenever you want everyone to stop and look at you.

2. Demonstrate the signal.

3. Explain that when you give this signal, everyone should:

    *   Freeze.

    *   Look at you.

    *   Listen to you.

4. Practice using the signal until all students comply within 5 seconds.

5. Review the signal as needed.

Signaling for Attention:

Getting students to stop, look, and listen.

Ideal Time: 5 seconds

1 Signal

Signal for student attention.

Use the signal before:

- Giving directions
- Providing feedback
- Students line up
- Students leave the cafeteria

2 Wait

Wait **5 seconds.** All students should be:

- *Silent*
- *Still*
- *Not touching others*
- *Looking directly at you*

Use your "I mean business" look with students who fail to comply quickly. (See "Ensuring Student Compliance" routine.)

Wait until you have everyone's attention before you give directions. Otherwise, some students may not hear the directions correctly.

Immediately praise students when they comply within the time limit.

3 Feedback

Immediately praise students when they comply within the time limit.

If students do not meet the 5-second goal, have them **practice responding** to the signal appropriately during recess, free time, after school, or during any other time that is inconvenient to the students.

Giving Directions

Rationale

Teachers spend many hours over the school year directing students, especially during transitions from one activity to another. The directions must be specific and clear. If they aren't, students cannot be expected to fully comply. Clear directions are:

- Specific and direct

- Given one at a time

- Followed by a 5-second wait period

When directions are vague or are interrupted, they often must be repeated. When they aren't repeated, students may be confused about what is being asked of them. The result can be chaos in the classroom. Students may begin to talk out, asking, for example, "What did you say? What page? Did you say only red crayons?" It is extremely important to have the attention of all students before giving directions and then to give the directions clearly.

Goal

To give specific and clear directions, so students will know what is expected of them.

Whenever possible, plan ahead to minimize "telling on the spot." Telling students on the spot makes it difficult to describe precisely what the students are to do and how they are to do it. By planning ahead, you can teach the students the simple steps you want them to follow and show them exactly what you expect them to do and how to do it. Planning out the steps for routines that you want students to follow throughout the year is critical. A well-planned routine can be taught to students in one session with minimum alterations. If you constantly alter a routine, your students will have a difficult time learning what behaviors you expect of them.

Give directions only after you have the students' attention. Break the directions into clearly defined steps, tell the students the steps one at a time, and demonstrate each step. Monitor the students practicing the steps and provide them with feedback on their performance.

Preparation

When writing your lesson plan, script directions so they are specific, clear, direct, in sequence, and can be easily followed. Before having the students practice, model what you are asking them to do. Then, as they practice, monitor their compliance. Continue practicing and monitoring until the routine becomes automatic. Monitoring student behavior is critical because:

1. It allows you to check for understanding or a possible breakdown in communication.

2 Students are more likely to comply when they know you are watching.

Training

Refer to the "Following Directions" Overhead.

1. Gain student attention by saying: "I need your attention" or using another signal you've taught the class.

2. Wait for compliance. Then continue with your directions. Say, for example, "Thank you! Please put your math books in your desk."

3. Give the next step: "Take out your spelling book and turn to page 15."

4. Wait for compliance. Then say: "When I see that everyone has their spelling books out and have turned to page 15, I will know that you are ready to begin the next activity."

5. Praise students when they comply: "Good job! I see that everyone has their spelling book out and is on the correct page. I am very pleased with how all of you listen and follow directions so promptly. Thank you."

In this example, the teacher gives students directions only after the students are paying attention. The students are then given defined steps to follow. The teacher watches as the students complete each step before telling them the next step to follow. Finally, the students are provided with feedback on their performance.

Avoid giving vague directions like the following, which are confusing and result in wasted time.

1. You begin without gaining student attention.

2. You speak rapidly while searching for something on your desk: "Okay, let's put our math books away and get out our spelling books. Also, put your notebooks away—but first make sure you have written down the homework. Turn to page 15 in your spelling books. I hear too much talking. I need you to put away your math books. Let's hurry."

In this example, the teacher fails to gain the students' attention before telling them what to do. As a result, many students will not hear the directions. The directions that are given are rushed and confusing for those students who are paying attention. Also, the teacher gives the steps in a random order, making it difficult for students to remember all of the directions. Finally, this teacher fails to monitor whether the students are doing the steps. Hence, minutes that could be spent on academics will be consumed by the teacher having to restate directions and reprimanding students for not listening and knowing what to do.

Giving Directions:

Getting students to understand and do exactly what you want.

Ideal Time: Approximately 10 minutes for the first time the directions are given and less than 4 minutes after students have learned the directions

① Signal

Signal for student attention.

Wait for all students to stop and look at you before you move on to the next step.

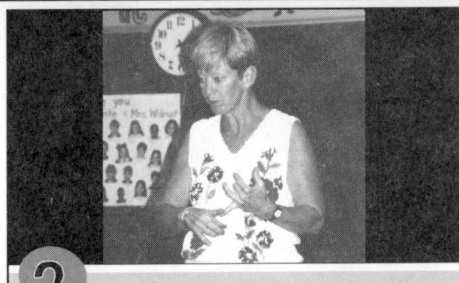

② Tell

Define **specifically** what you want the students to do, one step at a time. Start with: *"I need you to …"*

Academic Requests
I need you to:
  • Clear your desks of everything but your math book, pencil, and worksheet.
  • Write a heading on your paper.
  • Write neatly.
  • Write down the whole problem and circle your answers.

Behavior Requests
I need you to:
  • Sit quietly.
  • Raise your hand for help.
  • Use a quiet voice.

The first time you give a specific set of directions, use an overhead that clearly states the steps the students need to learn and do. (See "Student Training Overheads.")

③ Show

Demonstrate for students the appropriate steps for the students. Say, for example:

"When raising your hand for help, put your arm straight up like this. Wait quietly, and continue looking at the example on the board."

The first time you demonstrate a specific set of directions, give examples of both appropriate and inappropriate behaviors. For the latter, you could say:

"Behaviors that won't get you my help include waving your arm, calling out my name, groaning as you wait, and bothering others."

4 Do

Give students the **signal** and have them do the steps that you've explained and demonstrated.

The first time this step is performed with a particular set of instructions:

1. Check for student understanding by:

   • Asking a student to repeat the steps.

   • Asking a student to demonstrate each step.

   • Asking students to give examples of when and where the steps should be done.

2. Have the students practice the steps.

3. Have the students continue practicing until everyone is able to do all of the steps correctly two times in a row.

5 Monitor

Visually scan the classroom to see if all students are doing each step correctly.

Walk around the room, observing the students as they practice. If you see a student doing a step incorrectly, tell the student the correct behavior while you are in close proximity to him or her.

(Prompts are used to remind students of something they have forgotten or to assist them in doing a task. A prompt may be verbal or a gesture. Examples are:

"Remember to walk quietly to your desk."

"Completed spelling papers are to be placed in the spelling file."

The latter would be said while pointing to the file.)

6 Feedback

Give feedback after each step by telling students:

• Which steps were done correctly

• Which steps were done incorrectly

• Why missed steps are important

Tell and show students how to do any missed steps. Have the students practice during free time.

The first time you teach a set of directions, provide feedback by writing down the steps the students are doing correctly and/or incorrectly on an overhead transparency. Charts for this purpose are provided on the overheads in this book.

Providing Feedback

Rationale

Students depend on the adults in their lives to guide them in the right direction. Giving feedback is one form of guidance. Feedback provides students with information on their performance. Specifically, it informs students if they are performing as expected or if they need to adjust their performance. More important, it tells them how to make any needed adjustments. Without feedback, students may continue to practice inappropriate behavior or fail to perform up to expected criteria. Feedback can be verbal (praising students for a job well done) or written (giving a letter grade). Feedback is just that: feeding back to students how well they are doing.

Effective feedback is ongoing, specific, and related to the task. Feedback works best when it is immediate and frequent, and when the teacher's undivided attention is given to the student.

"Mary, I appreciate how you stopped immediately and looked at me as soon as you heard the signal. Good job!"

Goal

To give students feedback that is constructive and helpful.

You are the coach, guiding your students toward success. Give them feedback as they are doing what you've asked. Tell them when they are doing a good job, redirect them if they are off task, and prompt them when necessary. A smile may be all of the prompt a student needs.

Effective teachers use all three types of feedback. With regard to telling students when they are doing a good job, they may say, "I love how you are walking in such a straight line" to a class walking in a line as directed. Effective teachers also use feedback to redirect students who are not following directions correctly. To redirect students who are skipping in line rather than walking, they may say, "We are to walk in the halls. It is important that we walk together in line so we do not bother or hurt other students." Finally, they use feedback to prompt students who are failing to do what they have asked. Pointing to a messy table, they may tell the students, "This table needs to be cleared by the red group immediately."

It is helpful to provide students with verbal feedback about the accuracy of their performance when they are first learning to perform a task. However, nonverbal feedback is fun to do, and quite effective, after students have learned to do a task and no longer need instructional prompts. The Feedback Banks on the next page give examples of nonverbal positive and negative feedback that teachers may use.

Positive Feedback Bank: Verbal

Try not to say the same things over and over again. Vary what you say. Here are some examples:

- You're Cool!
- Super-duper!
- Excellent answer.
- You are on target.
- You are doing a wonderful job!
- Smart stuff!
- Very impressive.
- I love how you are always prepared.
- Way to go!

Positive Feedback Bank:
Nonverbal

- Smile
- Wink
- Give thumbs up
- Clap
- Nod your head
- Touch the student's shoulder and smile

Negative Feedback Bank:
Nonverbal

- Give a stern stare
- Give a thumbs down
- Shake your head from side to side
- Put your hands on your hips
- Stare at the student

Preparation

As preparation for giving feedback, think about which behaviors you want to increase in your classroom. Then practice giving feedback using the following model.

Model for Giving Feedback to an Individual Student:

1. **Look** the student directly in the eyes.

2. **Stand near** the student, at arm's length or closer.

3. **Turn your body** in the direction of the student.

4. Clearly describe the specific behavior you have seen or want to see.

5. Praise the student for using behavior you like, or redirect or prompt the student if his or her actions were inappropriate. Then **ask** if the student understands.

6. Check back to make sure the student is behaving correctly.

Training

Refer to the "Accepting Feedback" Overhead.

1.   Feedback When Students Are Doing a Good Job

It is important to praise students often every single day. Praise the behaviors you want students to increase (e.g., academic productivity and appropriate rule-following behavior). Praise students for following classroom rules, having good manners, staying on task, doing their homework, and so forth.

"Gayle, you're doing a nice job of following directions. I only need to tell you things one time and you do exactly as I ask. You are top-notch!"

"Chandran, you handed your homework in exactly on time and in tip-top condition. I can tell that you like your work to be neat. Your heading is written legibly, your paper is not wrinkled, and you numbered all of your problems. Keep up the excellent work!"

2.   Feedback to Redirect or Prompt

We all need redirection sometimes. Students should be redirected if they begin to stray off course, look puzzled, or were out of the classroom when directions were given. The majority of students will understand directions the first time they hear them if the directions are clear, few in number, and delivered on a level the students understand. However, depending on what was going on while the directions were provided, or on the difficulty of the task, some students may need redirection or prompting.

"Luam, I need you to turn to page 26 in your math workbook, not page 36."

"Donna, remember that during sustained silent reading the rule is no talking. It is important that the room is quiet so we can all read without distractions."

3. Corrective Feedback

As students are learning, they sometimes need correction. Corrective feedback should be given in a gentle, yet firm, manner. Don't allow students to practice incorrectly. Imagine learning to drive without receiving constructive feedback during the process. You would have a difficult and frustrating time.

"Deborah, let's look at the subtraction problem $5 - 3 =$ ___. First, draw five circles. Good. Now cross out three of them. How many are left? Good job! Now correct problems 2 and 3. Raise your hand when you have finished, and I will come back and check."

"Gary, I notice that you laughed when Billy wrote the wrong answer on the board. Laughing when someone is trying to work is not right. Billy needs the class to support him while he is learning, just like you need the support of your classmates while you are learning."

Providing Feedback:

Feedback about appropriate behavior will increase appropriate behavior!

Feedback should be given as students are performing a task or immediately after they have performed the task.

Ideal Time: 1 minute

① Look

Look the student directly in the eyes.

Maintain eye contact the entire time you are providing feedback so that you know the student is looking at you.

② Stand Near

When providing feedback to an individual student, **stand at arm's length** or closer to the student and turn your body in the direction of the student.

When providing feedback to the whole class, **position yourself** so that all students are able to see and hear you.

③ Tell

Clearly describe the specific behavior you are commenting on.

Praise the student for using the behavior you like. You might say, for example:

"I like how you got ready in less than 2 minutes."

Redirect the student if he or she is acting inappropriately. Tell the student the correct behavior to use.

Prompt the student who is doing nothing. Tell the student the correct behavior to use.

4 Ask

After giving corrective feedback, ask the student if he or she understands.

Or

Check for understanding by:

• Asking the student to repeat the directions.

• Asking the student to demonstrate the directions.

5 Check Back

Check back immediately to see if the student is using the correct behavior.

Or

Give the student adequate time to complete some work on his or her own and then provide praise or redirection.

Providing Correction

Rationale

Students who have learned the rules for a routine and have practiced them must be held accountable for their actions. A strategy that is often effective for turning around inappropriate behavior is to overcorrect the problem. For example, if a student writes on the wall, an overcorrection strategy would be to have the student wash the entire wall, not only his or her writing. Another approach to overcorrecting inappropriate behavior involves requiring the student to practice an appropriate behavior that can replace the inappropriate behavior. For example, a child who grabs a toy from a classmate may be required to ask the classmate for the toy and then share it with the classmate.

Punishments such as these are effective because they "fit the crime." Sending students to time-out, sending them to the principal's office, or yelling at them would be far less effective. Also to be avoided are consequences that are too strict.

Always be sure the consequences fit the crime. In other words, if a student runs instead of walking in the halls, think about what the student is supposed to do. You might state the consequence as follows: "Students are supposed to walk, not run. Go back and start again, this time walking."

Goal

To keep correction simple and related to the desired behavior rather than related to the misbehavior. Whenever possible, respond to inappropriate behavior by teaching the appropriate behavior and providing practice. Remain calm while holding students accountable. When students are "caught in the act" and expected to do what is right, compliance is generally high.

Preparation

Most often, the way to overcorrect a problem is decided immediately after the problem occurrs. Be sure the solution is related to the problem. When misbehavior such as property damage occurs, pause and consider how the student can fix the situation. Then decide how the child can spend additional effort fixing more than the damage that resulted from the behavior.

Training

Refer to the "Accepting Correction" Overhead.

The overcorrection technique can be implemented in two ways: through rehearsal and through recovery.

Rehearsal Use rehearsal for less severe rule-breaking that doesn't harm people or property. Rehearsal involves:

- Providing the student with direction about the right way to behave

- Requiring the student to practice the positive behavior 2-3 times while you watch

Praise is withheld during rehearsal.

A student who turns in assignments repeatedly without headings when he has been taught to always use headings may be required to head 3-5 pages in his notebook in preparation for future assignments. The student must do this work during recess or during another nonacademic period. The student is told that he may go to recess after headings are written and approved.

One benefit from this type of overcorrection is the educational aspect of having the student learn and practice an expected behavior to replace the inappropriate behavior. Positive effects have occurred for many children when this routine has been used to correct a wide variety of inappropriate behaviors. For example, the practiced appropriate behavior (e.g., sharing toys with peers) often increases while the inappropriate behavior decreases (e.g., taking toys away from peers). However, if a child refuses to comply with your request during this routine, you will need to implement the "Ensuring Student Compliance" routine.

Recovery Use recovery when the environment is disrupted or property is destroyed. The point is that the student should experience the inconvenience created by his or her actions. Recovery involves requiring the student to restore the disrupted environment to its original state and adding an extra job. Praise is withheld during recovery.

A student who overturns her chair is required to return the chair to its original position, then straighten the chairs and desks in the entire classroom.

A student who spits water on the wall after taking a drink from the fountain is required to clean and dry a larger section of the wall.

For both types of overcorrection, have the student stop participating in any ongoing activity and carry out the consequence. The duration for the solution need not be long. A consequence lasting approximately 3 minutes can effectively decrease future problems if there is a good fit between "the punishment" and "the crime." After the student has completed the overcorrection procedure, have the student return to the activity that had been interrupted.

Providing Correction:

Be sure the punishment fits the crime.

Ideal Time: 10-15 minutes

1 Signal

Tell the student to "freeze."

Walk directly to the student.

2 Tell

Tell the student the rule or procedure that should be followed.

"People do not chew gum on school grounds."

"We always respect school property."

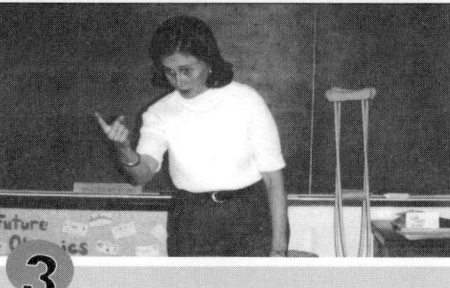

3 Rationale

Provide a rationale for the rule or procedure:

"Chewing gum is rude when talking. Students tend to throw their gum on the ground or stick it to desks which ruins school grounds and property."

4 Overcorrect

Tell the student that he or she will need to correct the situation caused by breaking the rule.

Assign a related task that will teach the student the effect of his or her actions.

A student who spits on the wall after drinking water is required to clean and dry the larger part of the wall.

A student who is putting gum under a desk is required to clean all the desks in the classroom.

A student overturning a chair is required to return the chair to its position and straighten the chairs and desks in the entire classroom.

5 Monitor

If possible, have the student overcorrect the misbehavior immediately. If this is not possible, do the overcorrecting procedure during recess, after school, or during free time.

Watch the student complete the task.

Redirect the student if he or she goes off task.

Check the student's work.

6 Feedback

Withhold praise during overcorrection.

After the student completes the work, review the rule with the student.

Convey an expectation:

"I expect that you will no longer chew gum at school."

Have the student return to the activity that had been interrupted.

Ensuring Student Compliance

Rationale

By far, the most important procedure for students to learn is to follow directions. When students follow directions immediately, there is more time to spend on academic learning and there is less time spent repeating directions or reprimanding students. When students fail to comply immediately after you make a clear request, the "Ensuring Student Compliance" routine, described here, is especially useful. With this routine, you use specific phrases (such as "I need you to...") and signals to clearly indicate that you mean business. Your words and actions show the students that they have only two options: (1) to do what you ask, or (2) to receive a consequence for noncompliance. Knowing that these are their only options will increase student compliance. If you practice this procedure carefully and consistently, students will be even more cooperative.

Using the phrase "I Need You to" to Gain Student Compliance

"David, **I need you to** walk to your seat and sit down quietly."

"Mary, **I need you to** circle all the nouns in the ten sentences."

"Ricardo, **I need you to** pick up the scraps of paper and put them in the trash can."

Goals

For students to comply with your request within 5 seconds. To consistently offer students (1) praise for complying within 5 seconds, (2) a warning if they fail to comply, or (3) a practice session that will be conducted during recess.

"The Look"

Grown men and women, years after having Miss Prim as their teacher, still grow pale when someone mentions her steely glare. Though Miss Prim was slight in build, her gaze, even from 20 feet away, carried the power and strength of a heavyweight boxer. That's because her "look" came from inside. It conveyed not only "I don't like what you are doing," but also "I am confident you will do as I ask so we can resume our lesson."

The "look" Miss Prim used is an effective way to get students to comply with directives. It works like this:

1. When a student fails to comply with a request you make, stop and give the problem your full attention.

2. With your face and body language, convey that you are serious but calm. Face the child directly, gaze steadily at the child, remain still, breathe normally, and above all, do not smile.

3. Say nothing. You have given your directions and nothing more needs to be said. Just remain calm and be fully committed to quietly wait for the student to follow your directions.

4. Monitor the time. The student must respond in no more than 1 minute but preferably within 10 seconds.

5. If the student does not comply, move closer, maintaining your stern look, tell the student what you need to see happen (use the phrase "I need you to"), and give one warning.

6. If the child fails to comply within approximately 10 seconds, apply your consequence for not following instructions.

7. At any time that the child does comply, thank him or her and continue the interrupted activity.

This strategy will work only if you are monitoring compliance, you remain calm, and you immediately apply the consequence every time a child refuses to comply after you have given the look and have said "I need you to..." Initially, children will need to learn that the look means that you fully intend to provide an aversive consequence. If a consequence is used every time, the look will serve as a quick signal to the students that you are serious and a consequence will be forthcoming.

You may want to practice the look in front of a mirror. Practicing can be a fun exercise for both shy and dramatic teachers.

Preparation

The best preparation for this routine—or, actually, for not needing to use it—is thinking before making requests of your students. You must consider whether the students have the skills necessary to comply with the request you intend to make. When students are not capable of complying, problem behaviors often escalate. After you make the request, you must consider whether the students have understood what you have asked. (See "Giving Directions" routine.) Finally, you must be ready with an appropriate consequence for noncompliance and be sure you can follow through. For example, if you tell students they are to miss recess, make sure you will be free to supervise them at that time. Otherwise, students will learn that nothing will happen if they don't do what you ask.

Training

Refer to the "Following Directions" Overhead.

Teach students to be alert to these key elements:

1. If any students do not comply with your request, you'll use the phrase "I need you to..." That phrase means *business*.

2. If the students do not obey, they will get one warning: "I need you to do ___ now or you will be practicing following directions during recess."

3. If the students do not obey after the warning, tell them they will practice during recess.

4. If the students still fail to comply, try the consequences listed in the box on page 59.

Ensuring Student Compliance:

Getting students to do what you want, when you want it done.

Ideal Time: 10 seconds

① Signal

Signal for student attention.

Wait for all students to stop and look at you before you move on to the next step.

② Tell

Tell the students what you want done:

"I need you to …"

• Give a clear request using these key words.

• Never state your request as a question (e.g., Would you please…?).

• Remain calm.

③ Monitor

Give the students 5–10 seconds to comply.

Watch the students as they do what you ask.

If the students do not comply, go to Step 5.

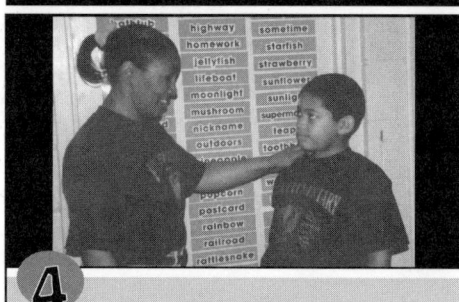

4 Feedback

Praise the students if they obey the request:

"Thank you for doing what I asked so quickly."

Resume the interrupted activity.

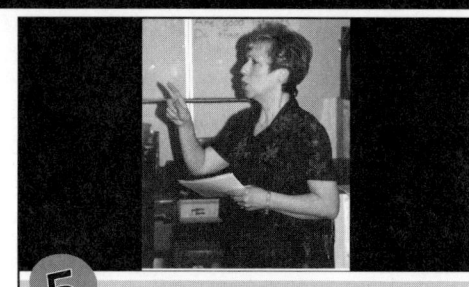

5 Warning

Remain calm.

Walk to the students who are not complying.

Look directly at the students.

In a very serious voice give the students a warning using these key words:

"I need you to _____ now or you will be practicing _____ during recess."

6 Feedback or Practice

Monitor for compliance. **Praise** the students if they comply.

If students do not do what you request tell them when they will practice:

"Tasha and Linda, you do not understand how to follow directions. You will need to stay in at the next recess to practice with me."

Apply additional consequences if the students continue to disrupt the class or are disrespectful. (See "Possible Consequences" box.)

Serious Behavior Problems

Serious behavior problems are relatively uncommon when teachers use the techniques described in this book. Most likely, your school has a schoolwide disciplinary system for handling such problems. For example, your school rules may state that the student will be referred to the principal's office or that a parent will be immediately called. The following are some possible consequences for behavior problems suggested by Rhode et al. (1993) that may not be included in your school's disciplinary system. We recommend considering their use. Another helpful resource is the *Teacher's Encyclopedia of Behavior Management* by Sprick and Howard.

Possible Consequences for
Serious Behavior Problems:

❏ Arrange with another teacher to send students who have committed a serious infraction to his or her classroom for 10 minutes.

  • Assign academic work for the student to do while in the other classroom.

  • Ask the other classroom teacher to direct the student to do the work. The student should not participate in fun activities.

  • If possible, send the student to an older classroom. An older classroom is preferable since students often enjoy watching younger children, which will make most children stay on task.

❏ Send the student to the principal's office with another student. The accompanying student will give a note to the principal about the child's infraction, report to you any messages from the principal, and inform you that the student has arrived at the office. Before re-entering the classroom, the student will need to apologize for the inappropriate behavior and write a plan for improving the behavior.

❏ Have the student sit near your desk for the day.

❏ Have the student call his or her parent(s) at home or work to report the problem, what he or she will do to improve the problem, and that a progress note will be sent home that day.

❏ Provide in-school suspension.

Adapted with permission from Rhode, Jenson, and Reavis (1993). *The Tough Kid Book: Practical Classroom Management Strategies.* Longmont, CO: Sopris West.

Grading on the Spot

Rationale

Academic performance improves when students know that they will receive feedback. The more immediate the feedback, the more effective it is. The quick correction of errors enables students to practice skills appropriately. Further, teacher review of student work provides the basis for making instructional decisions about reteaching. However, grading can take a lot of time. The "Grading on the Spot" routine, described here, and the "Student Grading" routine, described in the "Responsible Student Routines" section, provide immediate feedback while decreasing teacher time spent on grading.

Goal

To provide immediate feedback by correcting student work during class time.

Preparation

1. Write step-by-step directions for the work you want students to do on the board. Include examples for students to follow.

2. Tell the students which problems you want them to complete and that they should follow the directions and examples on the board. Explain that as they work you will be walking around, circling any incorrect problems on their papers, and helping them answer the problems correctly.

Training

Refer to the "Grading on the Spot" Overhead.

During the intial training session:

1. Prepare students for independent work by writing out the steps that need to be followed or by writing several examples on an overhead or the blackboard.

2. Tell students to refer to your steps as they complete their work.

3. Tell your students that you will check their work and will be circling any wrong answers on their papers.

4. Inform the students that they are to review the steps on the board and try to redo all the circled problems. If the problem is still difficult to do, have them raise their hands for help.

5. Tell students to work on other problems or work while they wait for help.

 You may want to give the students another chance to correct any graded papers that are returned to them. Students are then given additional practice on past skills. Students should have a learning task to do while waiting for the teacher's help.

Grading on the Spot:

Provide immediate feedback.

Ideal Time: 5 minutes

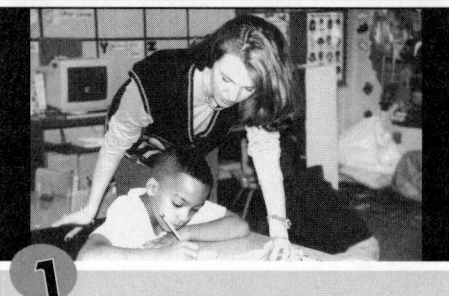

① Monitor

Write step-by-step directions on board and give examples for students to follow.

Walk around the classroom scanning students' work to see if it is correct.

Keep an eye out for students requesting help.

② Mark Incorrect Answers

Circle problems that are incorrect with a colored marker.

Write your initials next to the last problem that you checked. When grading completed papers later, the initials will indicate the problems you have already graded.

③ Reteach

One-on-one with the students, reteach any steps the students are completing incorrectly.

Prompt the students to review the directions and examples on the board for the steps they are completing incorrectly.

4 Review

After the students reattempt the problems, continue to review and grade their work.

If a student is unable to complete several problems correctly, review all of the steps with the student after the working time limit has passed.

If you observe that several students are unable to complete the problems correctly, stop the independent seatwork and review with the class the steps the students are consistently missing.

At the end of the working session, provide general feedback to both individual students and the class on their progress.

5 Complete Grading

Collect the papers. (See "Passing In Papers.")

Review the problems you'd marked as incorrect to see if the students corrected their mistakes.

Any of these problems that are now correct should be counted as correct.

Resume grading the papers with the problem after your initials, since your initials indicate that you have already reviewed the previous work.

 Intermittently provide rewards for corrected work to encourage students to rework incorrect problems.

Basic Student Routines

Requesting Assistance

Rationale

Sooner or later, every student will need help with something. Some students do not ask for help when they need it. Others request help for trivial concerns, wasting academic time. The "Requesting Assistance" routine, described here, provides students with guidelines for what are appropriate requests and with steps for getting your attention.

Goal

To teach students to appropriately request assistance, preventing their "acting out" for teacher attention.

Preparation

Determine the signal students will use to get your attention when they need help during independent seatwork, group work, or other school activities. You may decide to use different signals for different situations or areas. For example, students may use one signal when you are busy helping others, and may use another signal when you are free. See the "Student Signal Bank" box for signal ideas.

Training

Refer to the "Requesting Assistance" Overhead.

1. Tell the students the signal they should use when they need help.

2. Demonstrate the use of the signal.

3. Have the students practice using the signal.

4. Review the use of the signal as needed.

5. Remind the students about using the signal before beginning an activity such as independent seatwork.

6. Praise students for complying.

Student Signal Bank

Here are some ways students can get your attention:

*   Raise hand
*   Signal with a paper tube that is half green and half red. Students keep the tube on their desk with the green side pointing up. When they need help, they flip the tube over so the red side points up.
*   Signal with a card that has the word HELP written on it in bright colored letters. The card is placed in a clear plastic bag, in a pencil bag, or in sheet protectors, and the holder is taped to the side of the student's desk so that the blank side of the card is showing. Plastic sheet protectors can be purchased at office supply stores. When the student needs help, he or she turns the card over so that the word HELP is showing.

Requesting Assistance:
Getting students to signal for help.

Ideal Time: Less than 2 minutes

1 Monitor

After students know the signal for help, allow them to use it during work time.

Scan the room for the signal.

2 Respond

If a student uses the signal, walk to the student and determine what help is needed. Say, for example:

"Thank you for using the signal. What do you need?"

Provide assistance only for academic topics.

Continue to monitor all students.

Provide the needed assistance and direct the student to return to work.

 If the student requires more help than you can give in a few minutes, assign a tutor or provide assistance during free time.

3 Redirect

When a student asks for help without the signal or uses the signal incorrectly:

1. Say *"You are not asking for help in the correct way. You need to put the red color up. Go back to work. In 2 minutes, you may ask for help again. This time do it correctly."*

2. Do not talk, argue, or debate with the student.

3. When the student signals correctly, respond and provide assistance.

   If the student signals incorrectly a second time, assist the student but arrange for the student to practice using the signal during recess, free time, or another nonclass time.

Beginning the School Day

Rationale

You can jump-start the instructional day by having students follow a routine that brings order to the classroom first thing in the morning. With this routine, students have a set procedure for putting their school materials where they can be easily accessed, making sure their supplies are in working order, and getting to work on the day's assignment. Plus, while the students are occupied carrying out this routine, you have time to complete administrative duties.

Goal

For all students to put their book bags and materials in designated locations, check that their pencils are sharpened and other supplies are accessible and usable, and begin working on a posted assignment within 5 minutes of the morning bell.

Preparation

1. Post the daily assignment on the board or the overhead prior to students entering the classroom. Assignments should consist of work that students need to practice but can complete accurately with little assistance. (For ideas, see the "Daily Assignment Bank" box.) The work should take

approximately 10 minutes to complete, giving you time to complete the morning administrative duties.

2. Organize the materials you will need to teach your morning classes.

3. Pull together all the equipment and class supplies you will need (e.g., worksheets, materials for hands-on experiments, books to be read to students).

4. Go to the student line-up area before the bell rings so that you can make sure the students are getting in line quickly and quietly and instruct them about their morning tasks.

 Write the daily assignment on a transparency. Display it in the morning and then again at recess for those students who did not finish the assignment in the morning.

Training

During the initial training sessions, review the "Beginning the School Day" overhead with the class. For each task, follow the steps of the "Giving Directions" routine so that students know exactly how you expect them to behave when they enter the classroom.

Beginning the School Day:

Getting students ready for the instructional day and working right away

Ideal Time: 12 minutes

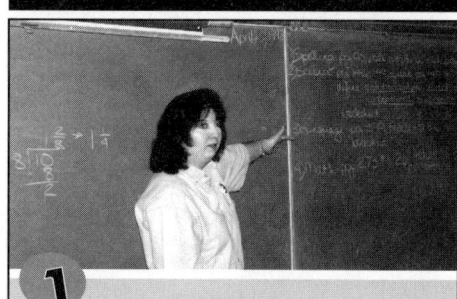

1 Post

Post the daily assignment before school begins.

Daily Assignment Bank

• Problems that review yesterday's work

• Instruction to complete yesterday's work

• Story starter

• Reading assignment

• Writing and/or spelling practice

• Instruction to use flashcards with a partner and then test each other

2 Stand and Signal

Before the morning bell rings, go to the student line-up area and monitor their line-up behavior.

Ten to 15 seconds before the bell, signal for student attention.

3 Tell

Tell the students what you want them to do, one task at a time. Say, for example:

"I need you to …"

• Put your coats and book bags in the closet.

• Sharpen your pencils.

• Begin the daily assignment.

• Place your homework, parent notes, and so forth, on the top right-hand corner of your desk.

Tell the students that they will have 5 minutes to complete this morning routine, sit at their desks, and begin working on the daily assignment.

Admit the students to the classroom only after they are quiet and in line and have listened to your instructions.

Once students have become adept at following the routine, you no longer have to state the tasks.

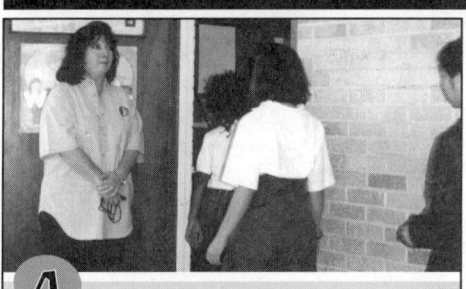

4 Monitor

Monitor the students as they enter the classroom and begin the morning routine.

- Visually scan the classroom.
- Walk around the room.
- Greet the students.

Use this time to collect homework and pick up any notes from home.

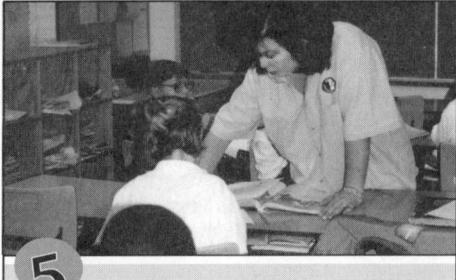

5 Feedback

Praise compliance.

When necessary, prompt students to pick up the pace.

Redirect students if they are off task. (See "Providing Feedback.")

If directions are not followed and/or students exceed the time limit, have students repeat the routine during recess or free time. Have them practice any steps missed.

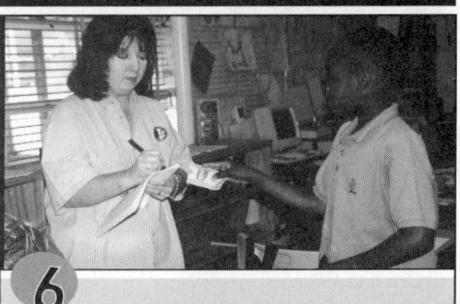

6 Administrative Duties

While students carry out this routine, take care of administrative duties, such as:

- Collecting lunch money
- Taking attendance
- Collecting make-up work
- Addressing parent notes and other communications

Sharpening Pencils

Rationale

Developing writing skills is critical during the elementary school years. As they learn and practice these skills, students will have more control and will be able to write more clearly and neatly if their pencils are sharp. By appointing one student to be the "Pencil Captain" who is responsible for sharpening a supply of pencils and then passing them out at set times during the day, you can avoid the classroom disturbance of numerous students getting up throughout the day to walk to the pencil sharpener. This routine ensures that a ready supply of sharpened pencils is always kept on hand.

Goal

For a "Pencil Captain" to be in charge of sharpening a supply of pencils for the class and, at specific times throughout the school day, replacing the students' dull pencils with sharpened ones.

Preparation

1. At the beginning of the school year, request that students bring in a supply of pencils.

2. Decide which student will be the "Pencil Captain." This person will be responsible for sharpening pencils for the class, passing out sharpened

Pencil Captain Responsibilities

1. Sharpen the pencils in the morning, during cleaning time, at the end of the day, or during a break.

2. Exchange dull pencils with sharpened pencils at set times.

3. Keep the pencil sharpener and surrounding area clean.

pencils to the students, and collecting the students' dull pencils. You may want to assign a different student each week.

3. Place the pencils in a pencil box near your desk or in another location that will be easy to monitor.

4. Provide each student with two sharpened pencils.

5. Determine times at which the "Pencil Captain" will exchange sharpened pencils for the students' dull pencils. Ideal times may be at the end of the school day and before recess, so students immediately begin working when they enter the classroom.

6. Decide the time of day when the "Pencil Captain" will sharpen the pencils.

Training

Refer to the "Sharpening Pencils" Overhead.

1. Explain to the students that you will appoint a "Pencil Captain" who will be responsible for sharpening and handing out pencils, and for cleaning up the pencil sharpener area.

2. Show the students where the pencil sharpener is kept, how it is used properly, and how to clean up the shavings.

3. Show the students where the pencil box will be kept and how many pencils should be in the box.

4. Tell the students when the "Pencil Captain" will sharpen pencils.

5. Tell the students when and how often the "Pencil Captain" will collect dull pencils and hand out sharp ones.

6. Go over the "Pencil Captain" responsibilities and appoint a Pencil Captain.

7. Tell the students that when you signal for them to check their pencils, they should look to see that they have two sharp pencils. If they don't, they should place their dull or broken pencils on the upper right-hand corner of their desks. Then the "Pencil Captain" will replace them with sharp pencils.

8. Tell, show, and practice how a "Pencil Captain" sharpens pencils and enchanges sharp pencils for dull ones. Have the students practice exchanging pencils.

9. Remind the students about the procedures to follow if their pencil breaks during the course of the day:

   • Use their extra pencil.

   • Raise their hand to request assistance should that pencil also break or become too dull. When you give them permission they should quietly walk to the pencil box to get a sharpened pencil.

Sharpening Pencils:

Preventing interruptions and unnecessary out-of-seat activity.

Ideal Time: Approximately 5 minutes

① Signal

At the beginning or end of the school day, or during a break, signal students to check their pencils.

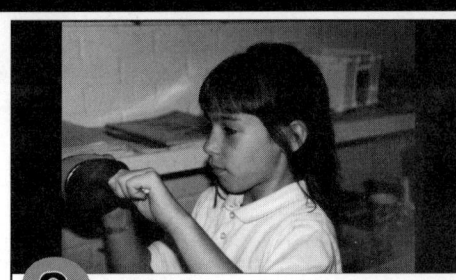

② Tell

Tell the students to place their dull pencils on the upper right-hand corner of their desk.

Remind the "Pencil Captain" that he or she should pick up the dull pencils and replace them with sharpened ones at your signal.

③ Monitor

Give students a moment or two to check whether they have two sharpened pencils in their desks and to place their broken or dull pencils on the upper right-hand corner of their desks.

When the students have completed this task, signal the "Pencil Captain" to pick up the dull pencils and replace them with sharpened pencils.

4 Remind

As the "Captain" exchanges the pencils, remind the students of what they should do if their pencil breaks during the course of the day:

- Use their extra pencil.

- Raise their hand to request assistance if that pencil breaks or becomes too dull.

- Quietly walk to the pencil box to get a sharpened pencil when you give permission.

5 Feedback

Praise students for complying.

If students do not refurbish their pencil supply appropriately:

- Have them practice getting out their dull pencils and placing them on their desks.

- If a persistent problem occurs with this procedure, direct students to sharpen all pencils during free time or recess and clean the pencil sharpening area.

 Monitor student requests for a new pencil (that is, pencils requested in addition to those the "Pencil Captain" provides).

If certain students are frequently requesting pencils, check to see if they are appropriately exchanging their pencils.

Ending the School Day

Rationale

Two important things have to happen at the end of each school day. Students need to write down and become clear about their homework assignments, and they need to spend a short time straightening the classroom to provide a smooth transition to a new day. The "Ending the School Day" routine, described here, provides a structure for doing both quickly and systematically.

A few words about homework are in order. Homework is assigned to strengthen academic productivity and to establish a firm skill foundation. After students have been taught a skill and practiced the skill with guidance, they need to be given the extra practice homework provides to reinforce their learning. When assigning homework, it is important to give very clear directions and provide students with the opportunity to ask questions. Further, because many students have problems remembering their homework assignments and parents often are not informed of the assignments and thus are unsure of what their child needs to practice, homework notebooks (in which students write down their assignments) are a good idea. Having students maintain a homework notebook, and monitoring their use of it, will ensure that they have accurate daily written information to refer to and to show their parents.

Goal

To have students own responsibility for two major activities: their homework and classroom cleaning.

Preparation

**Homework Notebook
September 12**

Math—Do problems 1–15, p. 5.
English—Do problems 1–10, p. 10.
Spelling—Study words on p. 9.

*Steve did great today in math! He finished all 10 problems correctly.
MP*

Ms. Prim, thanks for your note. Steve earned extra TV time for the good work.

1. Instruct each student to bring in a notebook for writing down homework assignments. The notebook should have a pocket for loose homework sheets. Tell the students to bring the notebook to school and back home every school day.

2. Explain that you will list homework assignments, the homework materials the students will need to take home, and the materials to be brought back to school on the board.

3. Tell the students that you will assign a "Homework Captain" each day, who will signal you 10 minutes before the end-of-day bell rings. You will then explain the homework to them and they will write the assignment in their notebooks.

4. Send a letter to parents explaining that the students will be writing down their homework assignments at the close of each day in a homework notebook and that the notebooks will be checked to make sure the assignments are written correctly. Let the parents know that you'll also use the homework notebook to communicate with them. Encourage them to review the assignments and monitor their children's work. Also encourage

them to use the notebooks for communicating with you. A sample letter is included as Figure 1.

5. Appoint a "Homework Captain" each day. In addition to signaling you 10 minutes before the end of the school day so you can go over the homework assignments, the "Homework Captain" will make sure the students have copied down the assignments correctly.

6. Prepare a class roster. Instruct the "Homework Captain" to put a check by the students' names after checking to be sure they have written the homework assignments correctly in their notebook.

7. Tell and show students the procedures for copying their assignments and getting their materials ready to take home.

8. Explain that writing their assignments and gathering their materials should take no more than 5 minutes. The remainder of the time should be spent cleaning their desks and areas of the room assigned to them.

9. Review with students the procedures for cleaning the classroom.

Training

Refer to the "Ending the School Day" Overhead.

Train all students on all steps of the routine and also on how to be "Homework Captains."

Homework Captain Responsibilities

1. Signal to the teacher when there are only 10 minutes remaining in the school day.

2. After the teacher explains the homework assignments to the students, write your homework assignment in your notebook. The rest of the class will also be doing this.

3. Walk to each student's desk and check to see if the students have written down the assignments correctly.

4. If they have, put a check next to their name on the class roster the teacher has provided. If they have not, have the "Homework Captain" help the student write it correctly. A blank is left on the class roster until it is written.

Dear Parents,

This note is about homework. Homework helps students practice the skills taught in class so that they can accomplish their work accurately and quickly. These skills are the building blocks for the more advanced skills they will be learning throughout the year. Unfortunately, many students forget to write down their homework assignments or to bring home the materials they will need to do their homework.

To prevent these problems, I am asking that each student bring a small homework notebook to school. The students will write down their homework assignments in these notebooks. We will check that each student has written down the assignments correctly. The students will then take the notebooks home with them to refer to as they do their homework.

The homework notebook can also be helpful to you. First, you can check the notebook every day to see if your child has completed all of his or her homework. Second, you can write quick notes to me in the notebook. I might also write quick messages to you in the notebook.

Your support in this homework program is appreciated. If you have any questions, please feel free to contact me. Please also help your child remember to bring the notebook, and his or her homework, back to school each morning.

Thank you,

Miss Prim

Figure 1: Sample letter to parents explaining use and purpose of homework notebooks.

Ending the School Day:

Getting students to prepare for their homework and straighten the classroom before going home.

Ideal Time: 10 minutes

1 Post Assignments and Homework Materials

Post all the homework assignments and materials the students will need to take home in a place that is visible to all students.

2 Signal

The "Homework Captain" will signal you 10 minutes before the end-of-school bell.

3 Tell

Go over the assignments and materials with the students and remind them to write the assignments in their homework notebooks.

Have the students take out the homework materials they will need to take home.

Ask the students to place their notebooks on the corner of their desks for the "Homework Captain" to check and then to put their notebooks and homework materials in their backpack or book bag.

Prompt the students to clean their desk area and assigned classroom area.

Also let students know how much time they have to clean.

 Assign to each row a specific cleaning task or classroom area.

 ## 4 Monitor

Monitor the "Homework Captain" as he or she walks to each student's desk and checks the notebooks.

Scan for proper cleaning behaviors.

Redirect students who are off task.

If students have a history of forgetting to bring their homework to class, put a star in the homework notebook next to the assignments that were received for each day. Then, suggest to the parents that the student earn a reward or activity at home for a specific number of stars.

You can also have students earn homework stars for work done in class. After 10 to 15 of those stars, you can reward the student with a free homework night.

 ## 5 Feedback

Praise appropriate behaviors.

If students do not follow the routine correctly, set a nonclass time to practice, such as during recess.

Free Time Activity Bank

If there is extra time at the end of the day, use the time for a review of the day's lessons.

- Conduct an oral question-and-answer session.
- Have the students ask one another questions.
- Have the students write in their journals.
- Have the students help one another study or correct one another's work.

Students can also use this time to check out and return library books.

Responsible Student Routines

Independent Practice

Rationale

After students have acquired a skill taught in the classroom, they need to practice the skill so that they can perform it quickly and efficiently. The faster a student is able to do a skill, the better he or she will be able to apply the skill and retain it over time.

As students practice on their own, it is important to provide them with input. Independent practice is a time to check for student understanding and provide feedback so that students practice skills correctly.

Goals

For students to work quietly at their desks on academic assignments. For the teacher to check student understanding and provide feedback and assistance.

Preparation

1. Remind the students of the signal they should use to get your attention when they need your help. (See "Requesting Assistance" routine.)

2. Have the students practice using the signal.

3. Teach the students the signal they should use when they have finished their independent work.

Using Cue Cards to Indicate Progress on In-Class Work

Give each student three cards—one green, one yellow, and one red. As the students work independently, have them place the cards on their desks, as follows:

The GREEN card means: "I'm working."

The YELLOW card means: "I need your help."

The RED card means: "I'm finished."

Positive Seatwork Behaviors

Stay in your seat.

Work quietly.

Keep your eyes on your own work.

Signal for help when you need it.

Check your work. Make sure you have followed each step correctly.

Signal when you are finished.

Do a freetime activity. (See "Free Time Behavior" routine.)

4. Have the students practice using the signal.

Training

Refer to the "Independent Practice" Overhead.

1. Tell, show, and have the students practice the seatwork behaviors you expect.

2. Teach the "Free Time Behavior" routine to the students so that they do not disrupt the class when they complete their work early.

Independent Practice:

Providing students with the opportunity to practice.

Ideal Time: Less than 15 minutes

1 Check for Understanding

Before assigning independent seatwork, check for student understanding of the skill to be practiced:

- Ask several questions about how the skill is used
- Have students answer the questions in choral response
- Ask for volunteers to demonstrate the skill

2 Tell

Tell and model what you want the students to do. As you do so, break the problems down into small steps.

Go over one or two practice problems, step-by-step, with the students.

Write the assigned problems and/or page numbers on the board.

How to Break Down an Addition Problem Into Small Steps for Students to Follow

1. Look at the operation.
$$\begin{array}{r} 23 \\ + 14 \\ \hline \end{array}$$

2. Look at the ones column.
$$\begin{array}{r} 23 \\ + 14 \\ \hline \end{array}$$

3. Add the numbers in that column.

4. Write the number under the column.
$$\begin{array}{r} 23 \\ + 14 \\ \hline 7 \end{array}$$

5. Look at the tens column.
$$\begin{array}{r} 23 \\ + 14 \\ \hline 7 \end{array}$$

6. Add those numbers.

7. Write the number under the column.
$$\begin{array}{r} 23 \\ + 14 \\ \hline 37 \end{array}$$

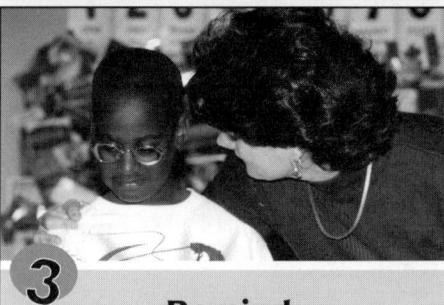

3 Remind

Remind the students how to behave during independent practice.

4 Set Time Limit

Estimate how long it will take the students to complete the work.

Tell the students how long they will have to complete the work.

Set a timer.

Say, "Begin."

5 Monitor

Walk around the classroom to monitor students working and the accuracy of their work.

Position yourself so you can monitor off-task behavior as you are helping students.

Redirect students who are off task.

Praise students who are working as instructed.

 You can help students work independently by:

- Indicating steps they are doing incorrectly.
- Modeling how to do those steps correctly.
- Checking back with the students to see if they are now doing the work correctly.

6 Feedback

After the timer rings, check to see who has completed the work in the time allotted. You may want to have the students grade their seatwork or pass in their papers. (See "Student Grading" and "Passing in Papers" routines.)

Praise students who had proper seatwork behavior for compliance.

Praise students for good work.

Give extra work to students whose behavior was off task, or have them practice any appropriate seatwork behaviors during recess or free time.

Student Grading

Rationale

Training students to grade their own work will increase their academic progress. The students receive immediate feedback on whether their answers were correct or incorrect. Moreover, you can quickly evaluate whether you need to teach the skill in a different way, need to provide more practice of the skill, or can turn your attention to teaching a new skill. With this routine, work is graded quickly by the students and then checked to ensure that they are grading accurately.

Goal

To have students grade their own work as a means of monitoring their progress.

Preparation

Have students bring red pens to school or have red pens available.

Training

Refer to the "Student Grading" Overhead.

1. Discuss with the students the importance of grading papers correctly. Explain that by accurately grading their work they will be able to learn whether they are following the steps of a procedure correctly. When they

have a number of wrong answers, they can request help. You and they can then find out if they are (a) applying the steps incorrectly, (b) making careless or random errors, or (c) need more practice with a prerequisite skill.

2.   Tell the students that you want them to use their red pens only for grading.

3.   Have the students practice marking a "C" by correct answers with their red pens.

4.   Have the students practice circling incorrect answers with their red pens.

5.   Assign a student to call out the answers to an easy assignment from the teacher's manual.

6.   Tell students that you want them to quietly raise their hands if they do not hear an answer that is called out.

7.   Demonstrate and provide practice in grading the assignment.

8.   If you would like students to swap papers for grading, tell them how you want them to exchange their papers and have them practice doing so. They should try to exchange their papers in under a minute.

Student Grading:

Enabling students to gauge their own progress.

Ideal Time: 5 minutes

1 Direct

Signal students to clear off their desks except for their red pens and the papers to be graded.

Tell the students whether they will be grading their own papers or swapping papers with another student.

Give the signal to exchange papers if appropriate.

Tell the students to write their names at the bottom of the paper they will be grading.

2 Provide Answers

Provide the class with answers by:

- Calling out the answers to the class
- Showing the answers on the overhead
- Having a student call out the answers

Monitor for raised hands, indicating that a student has not heard an answer. If a hand is raised, repeat the answer.

Have the students mark correct answers with a "C" and circle the incorrect answers.

3 Record

After they finish marking their papers, tell the students to count the number of correct answers and write that number at the top of the paper.

4 Collect

If papers have been exchanged, have the students return the papers to their owners.

Tell the students to look at their papers and circle or write down any concerns they might have about the grading or their work using their red markers.

Tell the students to pass their papers in. (See "Passing In Papers" routine.)

Direct the students to put their graded papers on the upper right-hand corner of their desks. Then, as you walk around helping students during the next seatwork activity, write the grades in your grade book.

5 Spot-Check

Randomly select several papers and check to see that they were graded correctly.

If they were, praise the students who graded them.

(Intermittently provide rewards, such as points or stickers.)

If any were not graded correctly, set a time to meet with the student grader and review the routine.

Have the students correct papers at the end of the day, as a homework assignment, or when they complete other work early.

Passing In Papers

Rationale

Checking student work regularly and providing feedback are essential to monitoring academic progress. This procedure takes the guesswork out of checking papers and is designed to be a real time saver.

Goal

For students to quietly pass in all requested materials and place them in a designated spot within 2 minutes.

Preparation

1. Decide on the heading you want students to use for all of their papers. For instance, you could have them write, at the top right corner, their name, the date, the subject, and the assignment or page number. (Some teachers also have students write down the number that corresponds to their name in the grade book. Using this number makes it easy to find student names when recording their grades.)

2. Prepare an area for students to place papers for your review, such as a shelf, basket, or file.

3. Choose one student each week to be responsible for collecting papers and placing them in the designated location.

Training

Refer to the "Passing In Papers" Overhead.

1.   Explain to students what should appear in the heading of their papers.

2.   Have the students practice writing their heading quickly and neatly. You may want to give them a set time limit. Writing headings should be done quickly so that the procedure does not consume more than a moment of academic time.

3.   Tell and show students the procedure for passing in papers: waiting quietly for the papers in their row to be passed to them, accepting the papers, adding theirs to the top of the pile, and passing the pile to the right.

4.   Since a different student will be "Paper Captain" each week, tell and show all students the procedure for quietly collecting the papers at the end of the rows and placing them in the designated spot for your review.

5.   Have students practice the steps using the "Passing In Papers" Overhead. Have them practice completing the steps within a 2-minute time limit.

Passing In Papers:

Getting requested materials from students quickly and quietly.

Ideal Time: Less than 2 minutes

① Signal

Signal for student attention.

Wait for all students to stop and look at you before moving on to the next step.

② Tell

Remind students to write the heading you've taught them on their papers. Say, for example:

"Make sure the correct heading is at the top right corner of your paper."

The heading may include:
1. Name
2. Date
3. Subject
4. Assignment/page number

Remind students of the procedure for passing in papers:

"Please quietly pass your papers to the right and stay seated."

③ Set Timer

Tell the students they will have 2 minutes and that you are setting the timer.

Set the timer for 2 minutes. Say "Go."

Students should begin to pass their papers to the right.

4️⃣ Monitor

As the students are passing in their papers, walk around the room and look to see that the papers are properly headed.

If any are not, arrange a time to practice with the student during free time or recess.

Visually scan the classroom. Make sure students are passing in their papers as directed.

5️⃣ Prompt Captain

After students have passed papers to the right, prompt the "Paper Captain" for the week to pick up the papers at the last desk of each row. Say, for example:

"Chris, you may pick up the papers and put them in the completed work file for spelling."

6️⃣ Feedback

Praise the students if they followed the directions.

If they do not complete the task within 2 minutes, repeat the routine immediately or have the students practice during recess, free time, or after school.

Putting Everything in Its Place

Rationale

Often, the reason students do not put things away is that they do not know where the materials belong. A well-organized classroom, with materials that are in good shape and easy to locate, runs smoothly. Once you have decided where you want materials to go, teach your students how you want them to retrieve materials, take care of them during use, and put them away. Having students put everything in its place, the procedure this routine addresses, is especially important when students are required to move from place to place in the classroom.

Goal

For students to quietly and quickly access the materials they need, use materials as directed, and put materials away after their use.

Preparation

1. Keep materials close to the work area in which they will be used. For example, keep art supplies at an art station.

2. Teach students how to access the materials they need and use them appropriately.

3. Teach students how you want them to put the materials away and clean their work stations.

4. Assign specific students to "captain" each work area. Each assigned student will:

    - Pick one helper if needed.

    - Look and listen for your signal to use the area and materials.

    - Listen to your directions.

    - Remind the students at the station about the rules and directions for cleaning.

    - Clean or monitor the cleaning of the area and the putting away of materials.

Training

Refer to the "Putting Everything in Its Place" Overhead.

1. Signal for attention.

2. Tell the students what needs to be cleaned up and remind them of the rules for cleaning.

3. Show the students how each area will look when it is being used for an activity and how it should look when the activity is finished.

4. Point out the proper place for each material.

5. Remind the students of how they should act when cleaning up:

   - Talk quietly.

   - Put trash in bin.

   - Put materials away.

   - Hand in completed work.

6. Have the students practice cleaning the different work areas and putting away the materials. They should complete the task in 5–10 minutes.

Putting Everything in Its Place:
Keeping the classroom clean.

Ideal Time: 5 minutes

1 Signal

Signal for student attention.

Wait for all students to stop and look at you before you move on the next step.

2 Tell

Tell the students what needs to be cleaned and remind them of the rules for cleaning:

- Talk quietly.
- Walk.
- Put trash in bin.
- Put materials away.
- Hand in completed work.
- Return to your desks, sit, and wait quietly.

Inform the students of the amount of time they will have.

Signal them to start cleaning.

 Assign numbers to students corresponding to specific clean-up jobs:

Student 1 picks up trash.
Student 2 puts away materials.
Student 3 collects and stores work.
Student 4 straightens the furniture.

3 Monitor

Scan for compliance.

Walk around room and look to see that students are following your directions.

At the end of the cleaning time, signal for student attention. Tell the students to get out their materials for the next class or to wait quietly while you look to see if all areas are clean and all materials are in the correct places.

 On a chart displayed where everyone can see it, put a mark next to each student's or group's name if they have done their job correctly. Give the class free time if all students receive a mark.

4 Feedback

Praise students if everything is clean and in its place.

If an area is not clean:

- Tell the students how the area should look and where the materials should be.

- Instruct the students to complete the job either immediately or during recess.

- Set a time for the students to practice cleaning the area in the correct way and within the time limit.

Making Up Missed Work

Rationale

Each school day, students are taught new skills or practice previously learned skills to enhance academic performance. When they are absent from school, they often miss learning and practicing basic skills they need to master if they are to successfully perform higher level skills that will be taught in the future. Getting missed work to students who are absent from school helps them to keep up with the class. Because it is often difficult for teachers to organize makeup work for parents to pick up the same day it is missed, the following routine was developed. It makes students responsible for organizing the makeup work for their partners when they are absent. Employing students to organize assignments not only decreases the teacher time involved but also provides the absent student with a partner they can call if they need help.

Goal

For students to record the work done in class and homework assignments for their partners when they are absent and place materials the student will need to complete the work in a designated location to be picked up by a family member of the absent student.

Assign partners at the beginning of the school year. Whenever possible, pair students who live near each other. Explain to students that they will be responsible for writing down the daily work missed for their partners when their partners are absent from school.

Write the partners' names in your grade book or where you log the students who are absent so you can easily identify the student who should be in charge of an absent student's makeup work.

Preparation

1. Assign each student to a homework partner.

2. Prepare Absent Assignment Forms using Absent Assignment Reproducible 1 or 2.

3. Place the Absent Assignment Forms in a set location.

4. Consider providing students with Homework Partner Folders in which they can place worksheets and handouts the absent student will need.

5. Designate a location in which students should place their partners' makeup work at the end of the day.

Training

Refer to the "Making Up Missed Work" Overhead.

1. Tell the students who their partners are.

2. Tell and show the students where the Absent Assignment Forms are located.

3. Tell the students that they will be responsible for filling out an Absent Assignment Form whenever their partners are absent.

4. Tell the students that they should pick up a form at the beginning of the school day and fill out the form as each subject is taught.

5. Practice filling out a form with the whole class. (See Figure 2.)

6. Tell the students that they will gather together the absent student's books and materials at the end of the day and place them, with the form, in the designated area.

7. Show and tell the students how you want them to bring the materials to the designated area.

Absent Assignment Reproducible 1

Name: _Joel Collins_   Absent Partner: _Randy Flynn_

Date: _September 22, 1999_

1 Subject: _Reading_

We read pages _59 to 65_ in the book _Reading for Fun_

During seatwork, we worked on: _Reading questions 1 to 5 on page 66_

The worksheets we worked on were:

The homework we need to do is:

2 Subject: _Math_

We read pages _100 to 102_ in the book _Learning Math_

During seatwork, we worked on: _Math problems 1 to 15 on page 103_

The worksheets we worked on were:

The homework we need to do is: _in Math Drills do problems 1 to 10 on page 91._

3 Subject: _Spelling_

We read pages _____ in the book _____

During seatwork, we worked on: _practicing our new words with a partner_

The worksheets we worked on were:

The homework we need to do is: _Study for our spelling test on Friday_

4 Other things you need to know: _The field trip permission slip is due on Friday_

Figure 2: Example of a completed "Absent Assignment Form"

Making Up Missed Work:

Having students help each other stay on top of classwork.

Ideal Time: Less than 5 minutes

1 Tell

When taking attendance, remind the partners of absent students to:

- Pick up an Absent Assignment form.
- Place the form on a corner of their desk.
- Fill out the form as each subject is taught.
- Ask questions if they don't understand an assignment.
- Get an extra copy of any worksheets or handouts and place them in their partner's homework folder.
- Gather their partner's homework materials and place them, with the Absent Assignment Form, in the designated location at the end of the day.

2 Monitor

Observe students to make sure they are filling out the Absent Assignment Form over the course of the day.

Check that the forms are complete or **ask** the students to read what they have written on the form.

3 Provide Time

At the end of the day, provide time for students to:

- Complete the form.
- Gather the homework materials their partners will need.
- Place the materials in the designated location.
- Ask you any questions they may have.

4. Feedback

Praise the students if the forms are completed accurately and all the necessary materials prepared are gathered.

Redirect the students if the routine is not followed correctly. Provide practice during recess, after school, or during another free time.

5. Transport Materials

Direct the students to take the form and materials to the designated location.

Have the office notify the absent student's parents or a sibling to pick up the work.

Transition Routines

Transitioning

Rationale

Students change activities an average of 15 times per day. If each transition requires 10 minutes, students will spend 150 minutes of the school day getting ready for activities instead of working on academics. Moreover, the longer the transition, the more likely that behavior problems will ensue: Without structured time, students are more likely to engage in horseplay or misbehavior. With the routine described here, students will learn to make transitions quickly and in an orderly manner.

Goal

For students to transition from one activity to another in 4 minutes or less.

Preparation

1. Obtain a digital timer to use in the classroom. This timer will be used to set a time limit for each transition. The teacher will tell students what to do and estimate the time that it will take the students to do the required tasks. However, most transitions should be completed within 4 minutes.

Training

Refer to the "Transitioning" Overhead.

Since each transition will require the students to follow different behaviors, at this point you'll need to give the students only the following information.

1. Tell the students that they will need to notice your signal for attention. Remind them that they should stop what they are doing and look quietly at you when you give the signal.

2. Inform the students that you will then give them specific directions and a time limit for the task you want them to do.

3. Explain to the students that they should try to complete all the directions correctly within the set time limit.

4. Show the students the timer and how it will ring when the time limit has passed.

5. Demonstrate and practice each step with the students.

Transitioning:
Getting students to end one activity and begin another in a timely fashion.

Ideal Time: 4 minutes for most transitions

1 Signal

Signal for student attention.

Wait until you have the attention of all students before going on to the next step.

2 Tell

Tell students the academic task you want them to do:

"I need you to …"
- *Put away your spelling materials and take out your math books.*
- *Clear off your desks.*

Tell students how to behave during the transition:

"I need you to …"
- *Sit quietly while I . . .*

3 Time Limit

Can You Beat-the-Buzzer?

- Tell students how much time they have to get in ready position.
- Set timer.
- Monitor by walking around.
- Remind students of how much time is left.
- When students are ready, turn off the timer and tell students they beat the buzzer! Good job!

4 Monitor

Scan the room for student compliance.

Walk around the room prompting students who are off task.

5 Feedback

If the students complete the task before the time limit is up, say:

"You did a great job! I like how you got ready in less than 2 minutes!"

If all of the students do not complete the task before the time limit is up, say:

"Some of you did not get ready in the time provided. Next time I expect you will do a better job. Those of you who did get ready in time, good job!"

If needed, have students practice the transition steps during free time or recess.

6 Begin Next Activity

Start the next lesson.

How did you do?

- Did you gain and maintain student attention?
- Did you give clear, specific directions?
- Were the students able to do the task required?
- Did you use the monitoring techniques suggested?
- Did the transition take less than 4 minutes?

Breaking Into Small Learning Groups

Rationale

When breaking into small groups, students need to know specifically where they are to go, how they are to get there, and what is expected of them once they are there. This routine gives students a procedure to follow that will make breaking into small groups an orderly, rather than a chaotic, task.

Goal

To have students quietly break into their groups and be ready to work within 4 minutes.

Preparation

1. Determine how you want the class to break into small learning groups and which students will work together.

2. Decide where the students will work. Will they need to move their desks or will they walk to one side of the room?

Try these ideas for assigning students to groups:

Place a piece of tape with each student's name at a particular place on the floor and have the students find their spots.

Write student names on Popsicle sticks and pick sticks randomly from a jar to assign students to small learning groups.

Training

Refer to the "Breaking Into Small Groups" Overhead.

1. Signal for student attention.

2. Explain that, at times, the class will be breaking into small groups.

3. Give specific directions on how the students should break into their groups. For example, they should walk quickly and quietly to the designated area when their name or row is called, sit down, and look at you for direction.

4. Explain that you will tell the students the materials they will need to bring to their groups.

5. Explain that you will set the timer for 4 minutes, which is how long they will have to move into their groups and get ready for the activity.

6. Provide practice.

7. Monitor student movement and redirect students if necessary.

8. Praise the students if they complete the task within the time limit. If students do not complete the task in time, review the steps and provide additional practice.

Breaking Into Small Learning Groups:
Getting students to their working areas in an orderly manner.

Ideal Time: Less than 4 minutes

1 Signal

Signal for student attention.

Wait for all students to stop and look at you before you move on to the next step.

2 Tell

Inform students that they will be breaking into small groups.

- If you have not already done so, assign students to their groups.
- Indicate where each group will be located.
- Tell the students which materials they will need to bring to their groups.
- Let the students know what the activity will be. Remind students to walk to their work area quietly when you tell them to. Some teachers have their students move to their groups by allowing one row or area to move at a time.
- Tell the students how long they will have to get into their groups and ready for the activity.
- Set the timer and tell the students to begin.

Small Learning Group Rules

If necessary, remind students of the rules to follow when working in small groups:

1. Use a quiet voice.
2. Have only one person talk at a time.
3. Remain seated.
4. Stop all discussion and activity when the teacher signals and listen for directions.
5. Use the help signal when assistance is needed.

3 Monitor

Walk around the room as students move into groups. Redirect students as necessary.

Scan the room as the students walk to their groups, sit in their groups, and look at you for further directions.

 Give each student in each group a number that will indicate a specific job. For example,

    1 is a recorder

    2 is a reporter

    3 is a reader

    4 is a collector

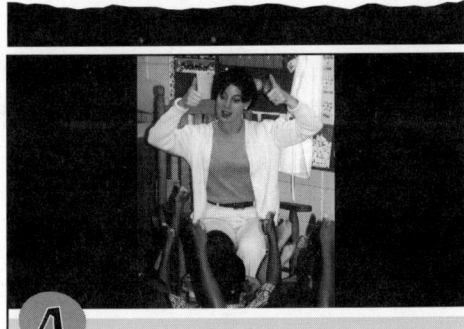

4   Feedback

Praise students if they accomplish the following within the time limit:

- Walking to their group areas.
- Sitting in their correct groups.
- Looking at you quietly.

If students do not follow the routine correctly:

- Inform the students that they will need to practice this skill.
- Set a time to practice that is inconvenient for students, such as during a free period.
- Have the students practice moving into their groups until they get it right.

Taking a Bathroom Break

Rationale

Although most teachers establish bathroom times and the majority of students use the bathroom during those times, students will sometimes need to go to the restroom during academic time. The following routine, established for just those times, will (1) allow students to use the bathroom without interrupting your teaching, (2) allow you to monitor the amount of time students are missing from class, and (3) allow you to handle bathroom misuse during nonacademic times such as recess or free time.

Goal

For students to sign out of class in a Bathroom Notebook, leave the class quietly, use the bathroom, and sign back in, all without disturbing the class, when they need to use the bathroom during academic time.

Preparation

1. Set up routine bathroom times during the day (e.g., before class, midmorning, during recess, during lunch).

2. Create a Bathroom Notebook in which students will write their name, the time they leave the classroom for the bathroom, and the time they return to the classroom.

3.   Place a clock near the notebook so students can easily see the time.

4.   Plan to examine the Bathroom Notebook periodically to determine if students are frequently going to the restroom during class time or spending excessive time there.

5.   For older students, consider appointing a "Bathroom Captain." The "Bathroom Captain" would be responsible for monitoring the notebook, making sure the clock is set correctly, and reporting any misuse of the notebook to you.

Training

Refer to the "Taking a Bathroom Break" Overhead.

1.   Teach students to follow the following routine when they need to use the bathroom during academic time:

   •   Walk to the Bathroom Notebook quietly without bothering others.

   •   Sign your name and write the time in the notebook.

   •   Walk directly to the bathroom without making noise.

   •   After using the bathroom, be sure to flush the toilet, wash your hands without splashing, and throw out any trash.

   •   Walk directly back to class.

- Write down the time you returned in the notebook.

- Walk quietly to your desk.

2. If you assign a "Bathroom Captain," explain that he or she will:

- Monitor the Bathroom Notebook to see that students sign it and fill in the times correctly.

- Write the correct time in the book if a time is entered inaccurately.

- Quietly tell students what steps they missed at the next transition.

- Notify you during recess of any missed steps.

3. Show and practice the steps with the class and "Bathroom Captain" (if one is being used).

Taking a Bathroom Break:

Preventing classroom disruptions.

Ideal Time: 5 minutes

① Monitor Exit

Note when a student leaves without interrupting your lesson.

Check the time.

Monitor if the student is:

- Walking to the notebook
- Not touching or talking to other students
- Signing out
- Walking out of the classroom

If needed, prompt the student to follow the rules correctly, have the student return to his or her desk and follow the routine correctly 5 minutes later, or set a time for the student to practice.

② Monitor Return

Note student's return without interrupting your lesson.

Check the time.

Monitor if the student is:

- Walking to the notebook
- Signing in
- Walking back to his or her seat without disturbing others

③ Feedback

If the student follows the rules, praise him or her for using the bathroom privilege correctly at an opportune time during the day.

If the student does not follow the rules, or was out of the classroom for more than 5 minutes without a satisfactory explanation, walk to the student and say:

"You have lost the Bathroom Break privilege until you can demonstrate the proper behaviors. We will practice during free time today."

Tell the student that until he or she demonstrates the proper behaviors during your practice session, he or she will need to ask for permission in order to leave the room. The student's Bathroom Break privileges will be restored once he or she has demonstrated the correct bathroom rules.

Set a time for the student to practice bathroom behaviors during recess or free time.

Lining Up and Walking

Rationale

At various times throughout the day, students need to move from the classroom to other locations. Getting students from Point A to Point B in an orderly, quiet fashion is critical for safety and the overall school climate. Without a system in place that includes supervision, students may get hurt and classrooms may be disrupted by noisy students.

Goal

For students to form a line and walk to the target destination in an orderly fashion without bothering other students and without wasting time.

Preparation

1. Determine where your students will need to walk during the day to get to physical education, music, recess, and so forth.

2. Walk from your classroom to the destination. Chart the quickest route.

3. If possible, avoid passing areas where there may be distractions, such as a P.E. class.

4. Once you have charted the walking routes, teach students the routes.

Training

Refer to the "Lining Up and Walking" Overhead.

1. Ask students to identify times and places during the school day when "lining up and walking" would be appropriate.

2. Define walking. (See box.)

3. Show students where and how you want them to line up.

4. Discuss the importance of safety and how this procedure will reduce the risk of students getting hurt or disrupting classrooms.

5. Tell, show, and practice:

    *   Walking slowly to line

    *   Standing behind a person in line

    *   Keeping hands and feet to self

    *   Remaining quiet

6. Have the students practice lining up and walking to another destination. Monitor their behavior.

walking (v): continuously placing one foot in front of the other in a slow pace while keeping hands and feet to self.

Lining Up and Walking:

Getting students quickly and quietly to a destination.

Ideal Time: Less than 4 minutes

① Signal

Signal for student attention.

Wait for all students to stop and look at you before you move on to the next step.

② Tell

Tell the students the destination:

"It is time to line up for art class."

If necessary tell students:

- What materials to bring

- How to carry the materials

- The route to take

Tell the students to walk slowly to the line as their names or groups are called, with no talking and keeping their hands to themselves.

③ Set a Time Limit

Say, for example:

*"You should be able to line up within 30 seconds. Remember to **walk**."*

4 Direct

Tell the students to stand behind their desks.

Direct them to line up.

Ways to Line Up

- Call out the months of the year, pausing between each. Have students line up according to their birthday month.
- Follow the same procedure for favorite colors, holidays, etc.
- Have students line up alphabetically by first name.

Avoid "Lengthy Line Syndrome"

- If you have more than 20 students, consider having them form two short lines. Then the lines pair up and walk side by side. This will make it easier to monitor the routine.

5 Monitor

Scan the students as they comply with your directions.

Walk around the room and beside the line. Redirect students when necessary.

When outside the classroom, try to position yourself so that you can see all students at all times, including when they are going around corners.

Corner Concern

If the walking route includes corners, position yourself at the corner so that you can see the students turning the corner, the students at the beginning of the line, and the students at the end of the line.

6 Feedback

Praise students if they follow the routine correctly.

If they do *not* follow the routine correctly:

- Have the class return to the classroom and restate the steps.
- Set a time to practice that it is inconvenient for the students, such as during free time.
- Have students repeat the routine.

Getting Ready for and Returning From Recess

Rationale

By having students stop their work a few minutes before recess and get the materials together that they will need after recess, you can prevent "the big stall" that all too often occurs following recess. This routine provides a procedure for students to start to work without delay when they return to class from recess.

Goals

For students to put away the materials they had been using and take out the materials they will need after recess so they can immediately get to work when recess is over. For students to quickly transition to the "working student posture" after organizing their materials.

Preparation

Prepare worksheets for students to work on immediately after recess.

Working Student Posture

Students will:
- Have the correct materials on their desk.
- Be looking at their work with their feet on the floor and their hands on the desk.
- Be reviewing, reading, or writing quietly as instructed by the teacher.

Back-from-recess activities can include:

- Timed drill sheets
- Practice drills with a partner
- Quiet reading of student choice

- Student writings
- Crossword puzzles
- *Weekly Reader*

Training

Refer to the "Getting Ready for and Returning From Recess" Overhead.

1. Tell the students that they will be practicing a way to prepare for recess and a way to return from recess. Explain that if they follow this routine you won't have to cut into their recess time to have them get ready for class activities.

2. Tell the students that they will have 2 minutes to get ready for recess.

3. During the 2 minutes, they should clear their desk except for a pencil.

4. The student who is responsible for collecting dull pencils and handing out sharp ones will do so. (See "Sharpening Pencils" routine.)

5. At the same time, you or a student you designate will pass out a worksheet that the students should place on their desk. They should begin work on the worksheet as soon as recess is over.

6. Alternatively, you may make an assignment for other independent or partner work to be done after recess.

7. Tell the students that they should then wait quietly to be excused for recess, sitting in the "working student posture."

8. Explain and show students the "working student posture."

9. Demonstrate and have students practice the routine.

10. Explain that after recess they should walk quietly into the classroom, put away their coat and any other materials, walk quietly to their desk, sit down, and begin work.

Getting Ready for and Returning From Recess

Part 1: Getting Ready for Recess: Preparing students to begin working after recess.

Ideal Time: 2 minutes

1 Signal

Two minutes before recess, signal for student attention.

Signaling is sometimes more effective when recess is mentioned.

"We have a few tasks to do before the bell rings for recess. If everyone listens carefully, we will be able to leave the classroom right when the bell rings."

2 Tell

Tell the students to prepare for recess by:

- Clearing their desks except for a pencil.
- Following the "Sharpening Pencils" procedure.

3 Assign Work

Pass out worksheets to students or assign the work they are to do after recess.

④ Monitor

Walk around while passing out the worksheets.

Scan the room. If any students are not preparing for recess, prompt them to clear off their desks.

Before letting students go to recess, make sure they are quiet, have work on their desks, and have a sharp pencil.

Excuse students for recess when all students are ready.

Getting Ready for and Returning From Recess

Part 2: Returning From Recess: Getting students immediately back into classwork.

Ideal Time: Less than 1 minute

5 Tell

Before entering classroom, remind students that they will have 1 minute to:

• Walk to their desks quietly

• Put away their coats and any extra clothing or materials

• Begin working

6 Monitor

Set timer for 1 minute.

Scan for compliance.

Walk around the room.

7 Feedback

Praise students if they get to work within 1 minute.

If a student is not working after 1 minute, redirect the student. Set a time for the student to practice promptly getting to their seat and working at free time or recess. Say, for example:

"John, I need you to be working immediately after recess. We will practice getting to work quickly during free time today."

8 Administrative Duties

Use the time students are working to:

• Prepare for the next class activity

• Check previous work

• Handle student problems

Special Behavior Routines

Welcoming Visitors

Rationale

Many schools allow visitors to enter classrooms at any time. Although having visitors is important, it can disrupt important instructional time. Unless the visitor is scheduled, your first priority is to continue teaching. You should wait until the lesson is completed or you reach a good stopping point to give the visitor your full attention. How can you continue teaching and still make visitors feel welcome? It's easy. Just follow this routine.

Goal

To have a student "Ambassador" greet unannounced visitors, show them where to sit, and provide them with a Greeting Letter so that you can continue teaching but know that the visitors have been made welcome.

Preparation

1. Each week, appoint a different student to be the classroom "Ambassador."

2. Designate a place in the classroom for visitors to sit.

3. Put together a one-page letter for visitors (see box).

Dear Visitor:
Welcome to Miss Prim's Classroom. Please make yourself comfortable. My teacher is presently busy teaching. As soon as she reaches a good stopping point, she will greet you. For now, please relax and feel free to watch us learn.
Thank you,
Malcolm
Student "Ambassador"

Training

Refer to the "Welcoming Visitors" Overhead.

1. Train all students to be "Ambassadors" and rotate this honor position on a weekly basis.

2. Show the students where visitors are to be seated. Explain that the "Ambassador" for the week is responsible for keeping the visitor area clean.

3. Tell the students that the "Ambassador" is to quietly walk to the door when someone knocks or enters the room.

4. Demonstrate how the "Ambassador" is to quietly and politely greet the visitor, saying, "Hello, I would like to welcome you to our class" and shaking the visitor's hand.

5. Demonstrate how the "Ambassador" is to quietly and politely show the visitor where to sit and give the visitor the Greeting Letter. Teach the students to use words like: "My teacher will be with you soon. Please have a seat while you wait and read this note. Thank you for waiting."

6. Demonstrate how the "Ambassador" is to thank the visitor for being patient.

7. Provide practice on the "Ambassador's" role.

8. Explain that the rest of the class should continue working or listening to the lesson.

THE "AMBASSADOR'S" GREETING

(said in a quiet voice):

"Hello. I would like to welcome you to our class. My teacher is busy right now, but here is a letter for you to read. Please have a seat while you wait. Thank you for waiting."

---

9. Tell the class that, at a stopping point, you will give them directions on what you want them to do while you are meeting with the visitor.

10. Explain that they should listen to the directions quietly and raise their hand if they have any questions.

11. Tell the students that they are to work quietly on the assignment while you are meeting with the visitor.

12. Demonstrate how the class should behave when visitors arrive and have the students practice the steps.

Welcoming Visitors:

Helping visitors to feel welcome without interrupting the lesson being taught.

Ideal Time: 1 minute

① Continue Teaching

Observe the visitor and continue teaching.

Do not stop your lesson until it is convenient to do so.

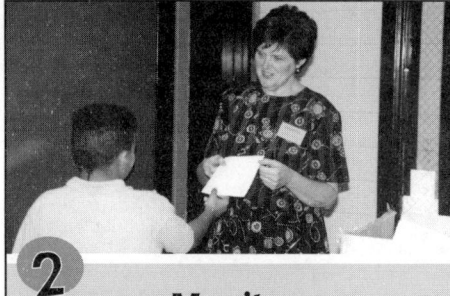

② Monitor

Monitor the "Ambassador" as he or she greets the visitor.

Be sure the "Ambassador":

- Shows the visitor where to sit
- Provides the visitor with the Greeting Letter
- Returns to his or her seat

Prompt the "Ambassador" if needed.

③ Provide Work

At a good stopping place, assign students an academic activity related to the lesson you've been teaching so you can meet with the visitor.

Some suggested activities:

- Write five sentences about what we just discussed.

- Make up five questions from the reading. Swap the questions with your learning partner and write down the answers to the questions you've been given. Then check each other's work.

4 Tell

Tell the students to work independently and quietly on the activity.

Tell the students how much time they will have to complete the activity.

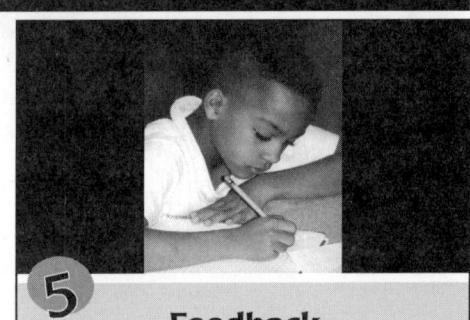

5 Feedback

After the visitor leaves, **thank** the "Ambassador" for greeting the visitor.

Praise the "Ambassador" for performing his or her role correctly or reteach any missed steps.

Praise the class for working quietly.

If the class did not remain quiet and working, set a time to practice this routine during free time or recess.

Free Time Behavior

Rationale

Providing students with free time in which they can choose from a set of activities has a number of advantages. For one, you can use free time as an incentive, with students earning it for working hard and progressing academically and losing it if teaching time is lost due to misbehavior. In addition, you use the free time period for meeting with students who need to practice academic skills, classroom routines, or social skills. Further, the activities you develop for free time can be used during recess on rainy days when students can't go outside to play. The following routine provides structure to free time periods.

Goals

For students to choose from a set of activities, obtain the necessary materials, and follow free time guidelines such as talking quietly, walking (not running), and cleaning up. for students to have time to catch up on or receive additional help with their academic work.

Preparation

1. Prepare a list of activities the students may choose from. This may include:

    • Homework completion

- Computer time

- Silent reading

- Peer tutoring

- Educational games

- Decorating bulletin boards

- Cleaning jobs

2. Provide locations and materials for the activities.

Training

Refer to the "Free Time Behavior" Overhead.

1. Tell the students when and how much free time they will have. You may want to make free time available when all students complete their work early. You can also have the class earn free time at the end of the day by working hard at their lessons.

2. Tell, show, and demonstrate how you want the students to behave during free time. Guidelines may include:

   - Walking to activity areas

   - Remaining in those areas until free time is over

   - Talking quietly

- Signaling for help

- Cleaning the area at your signal

- Walking back to their desks

Free Time Behavior:

Providing structure so students can have fun safely.

Ideal Time: 10 minutes for the activity and approximately 2 minutes for instruction and cleanup

1 Signal

Signal for student attention.

Wait for all students to stop and look at you before you move on to the next step.

2 Tell

Tell students why they are being given free time and how much time they will have.

Tell the students the activities they can choose from and:

- How to do them
- Where to do them
- How many students can be in each activity group
- How to talk quietly
- How to signal for attention

Set timer for 10 minutes.

3 Monitor

Scan for students who are not at an activity or are not participating in one.

Walk around room. **Redirect** students as needed. Say, for example,

"Jane, you need to be participating in an activity within 5 seconds."

4 Signal

When the timer goes off, signal and monitor for student attention.

Give cleaning directions. (See "Putting Everything in Its Place" routine.)

5 Feedback

Praise students if, after free time, everything is clean and in its place.

If the classroom is not cleaned:

• Tell the students how the room should look and where the materials should be.

• Tell the students to complete the job.

• Set a time for students to practice cleaning their activity areas correctly and the time limit you give. Have students practice during free time or recess.

Lunchroom Behavior

Rationale

Rules and expectations in the lunchroom are different from those in the classroom. However, many of the behaviors needed to get lunch, eat, return lunch trays, and so forth, are similar to behaviors expected in the classroom. For instance, lining up and walking (not running) are two common lunchroom routines that are also used in many classroom situations. The key to teaching lunchroom behaviors is to have students practice them in the lunchroom. This training allows students to become familiar with, among other things, how to obtain and return their lunch supplies. When students know and follow the lunchroom behavior expected of them, they have more time to spend relaxing and visiting with their classmates while eating their lunch. Moreover, the teacher's job will be to simply monitor students who are enjoying their lunch break in an orderly manner. The following routine can be used to teach students expected lunchtime behavior.

Goal

For students to arrive at the lunchroom on time, sit at the right tables, quietly eat their lunch, clean up after themselves, and exit the lunchroom as scheduled.

Preparation

1. Find out what supplies students will need at lunchtime in order to eat and then clean up. For example, find out how students should enter and exit the cafeteria, how to pay for lunch, how to go through the line, how to get utensils, where clean-up materials are located, and recycling procedures.

2. Adapt this routine to your own needs.

 Lunchroom Behaviors to Review With Your Students (if necessary, break down these behaviors into steps for your students to follow):

- Washing hands
- Getting lunch
- Paying for lunch
- Choosing where to sit
- Eating and visiting with friends in an orderly way
- Cleaning up
- Leaving the table
- Recycling materials, returning supplies, throwing away trash

Training

Refer to the "Lunchroom Behavior" Overhead.

1. Tell, show, and have students practice the behaviors they need to follow during lunch period:

    - Get your lunch supplies.

    - Line up for lunch.

    - Walk to the lunch room.

    - Walk to your table if you've brought your lunch.

    - If you're buying lunch, walk to the lunch line.

    - Get your food and pay for it.

    - Take your lunch to your table.

    - As you eat, talk quietly and remain seated.

    - No playing with your food.

    - At the signal, clean your table.

    - Throw your trash away, recycle materials, and return supplies.

    - Line up quietly and wait for instructions.

2. When using the Overhead "Lunchroom Behavior" to train students, you may want to add other behaviors, like:

    *   Always walk.

    *   Wait patiently when you are in the lunch line.

    *   Wash your hands in the designated area before you eat.

    *   Remain seated at your table until you are excused.

Lunchroom Behavior:

Having students eat and clean up in an orderly manner.

Ideal Time: 20-30 minutes

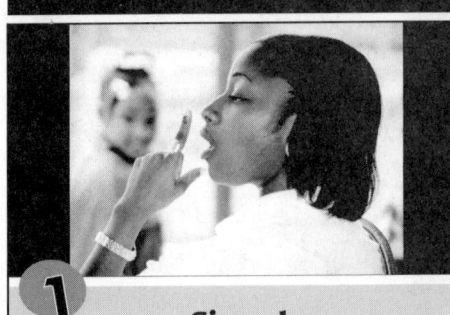

1 Signal

Two minutes before lunch period begins, signal for student attention.

Wait for all students to stop and look at you.

2 Tell

Tell the students to retrieve their lunches or lunch money and to line up quietly.

3 Line Up and Walk to Lunchroom

(See "Lining Up and Walking" routine.)

4 Monitor and Redirect

In the lunchroom, **monitor** the students to make sure they are:

- Walking
- Talking quietly
- Sitting at the table
- Eating their food without playing with it

Notice inappropriate behavior and redirect students as needed. Say, for example:

"Sally, you need to use your quiet voice."

5 Signal to Line Up

One minute before the end of lunch period, **signal** for student attention.

Scan to see if the tables are clean except for the students' trays.

If the tables are not clean, tell the students they have one minute to clean the tables.

6 Direct and Monitor

Direct the students to return lunchroom supplies, recycle materials, and throw out their trash. Explain that when they are finished doing that they are to line up quietly.

Direct the students to return to class.

Monitor students' walking behavior.

Behaving for Substitute Teachers

Rationale

Even the best students may misbehave when you are absent and a substitute teacher covers your class. Substitutes often have difficulty holding students accountable for their behaviors because they are with students for only a short time and don't know the classroom routines. The routine described here will inform substitutes of the behaviors you expect of your students and will hold students accountable when you are absent.

By practicing appropriate behaviors with your class, providing the students with an incentive for using these behaviors when substitutes teach the class, and by informing students that the substitutes will provide you with immediate feedback on the class's behavior, you can help motivate your students to be on their best behavior when you are absent. Moreover, by employing students to assist the substitute with finding classroom materials and conducting daily activities, you can help ensure that the substitute's day will be organized and increase academic time. When you appoint well-behaved students to help keep the class on task and organize a smooth day for the substitute, you can help the substitute have a pleasant visit with your students and, most likely, have a substitute who is willing to return to the classroom in the future when needed.

Goals

For the teacher to provide the substitute with clear lesson plans, a packet of worksheets, a seating chart, and the teaching materials that will be needed. For a student to greet the substitute, help him or her with locating materials during the day, and familiarizing the substitute with the classroom routines. For students to behave well when a substitute teacher is present in the classroom.

Creating the Perfect Seating Chart
Take pictures of students and paste them on a seating chart with their names.

Preparation

1. Choose a student who is responsible, seldom absent, and courteous to be the "Substitute Spokesperson."

2. Choose other well-behaved students to be responsible for specific tasks or subjects. (See class schedule in Figure 3.)

3. Prepare a Substitute Teacher Folder containing seatwork and drill exercises that can be used to fill time gaps. The substitute can use them to keep the students productively busy.

4. Copy a fun puzzle for the students to work on whenever they have completed their assignments throughout the day.

5. Prepare a seating chart with student names and, if possible, their pictures.

6. Create a Teacher Pleaser Checklist (see sample in Reproducibles section) for your class.

The benefits of the checklist are that it:

- Clearly informs the substitute of the behaviors he or she should expect from the class

- Provides a means for the substitute to easily report student behavior to you

- Provides an opportunity for students to earn rewards

- Provides an opportunity for you to have students review and practice the behaviors listed

Time	Teacher will:	Students will:	Helper
8:00-8:15	• Take attendance. • Collect lunch money. • Collect homework and put it in the basket on teacher's desk.	• Work on worksheet provided in substitute teacher folder.	Maggie
8:15-9:00	**Reading** • Review vocabulary words, asking for definitions and sample sentences.	• Give definitions and sample sentences aloud.	Sam

Figure 3: Example of a Substitute Class Schedule and Lesson Plan

Time	Teacher will:	Students will:	Helper
8:15-9:00 (cont'd)	**Reading** • Teach practice reading on pages 134-145. • Have students write five questions about the story. • From those questions, select eight questions that you will have all students answer. • Have the students who wrote the questions write them on the board.	• Take turns reading out loud. • Write five questions. • Write eight answers.	Sam
9:00-9:30	**Spelling** • Have students study words from present spelling unit by writing each word three times. • Give students a practice test. • Have students grade their papers while you spell the words out loud.	• Write each word three times. • Take the test. • Grade the test.	Troy
9:30-10:10	**English** • Review verbs on page 45. • Direct students to do problems 1-20 on page 46. • Have students write ten verbs from their reading story. • Pick a student to make a list of all the verbs the class found.	• Read page 45 and answer substitute teacher's questions. • Do problems. • Find and write ten verbs from the story. • Share their ten words.	Kayla

Figure 3: Example of a Substitute Class Schedule and Lesson Plan (continued)

Time	Teacher will:	Students will:	Helper
10:10-10:15	**Transition** • Have students clear off their desks and get new sharpened pencils. • Pass out *Weekly Reader* for students to read after recess.	• Put dull pencils on desk. • Clean desk area. • Wait quietly to be excused for recess.	Miguel
10:15-10:30	**RECESS**		
10:30-11:00	• Conduct *Weekly Reader* lesson with the students.	• Take turns reading the stories out loud. • Complete any activities.	
11:00-12:00	**Math** • Have students work on the multiplication worksheets found in substitute teacher folder for 20 minutes. • Have students grade their worksheets. • Play BINGO with students (rules are on the overhead transparency).	• Complete the worksheets. • Grade worksheets. • Play BINGO following the rules.	Stacey
12:00-12:20	**LUNCH**		Maggie
12:20-1:00	**History** • Have students read pages 56-66. • Have students work on the worksheet found in the substitute teacher folder—prepared for the subject for 15 minutes.	• Take turns reading material out loud. • Complete worksheet.	Renee

Figure 3: Example of a Substitute Class Schedule and Lesson Plan (continued)

Time	Teacher will:	Students will:	Helper
1:00-1:30	**Physical Education** • Bring students to the gym at 1:00 and pick them up at 1:30.	• Line up when given directions. • Walk to and from the gym.	Greg
1:30-2:30	**Science** • Have students read pages 70-82. • Have students watch the video. • Have students work on the worksheet found in the substitute teacher folder—prepared for the subject for 15 minutes.	• Take turns reading material out loud. • Watch the video quietly. • Complete the worksheet.	Tanya
2:30-2:40	**Journals** • Have students write five sentences in their journal on what they learned today and how they felt they did today.	• Write five sentences.	Shano
2:40-2:45	**Ending the Day** • Have students get materials ready to go home. • Tell students that there will be no homework today.	• Put books or papers together. • Clean up desk area.	Maggie

Figure 3: Example of a Substitute Class Schedule and Lesson Plan (continued)

Training

Refer to "Behaving for Substitute Teachers" Overhead.

Training the "Substitute Spokesperson"

1. Model for the "Spokesperson" how to greet the substitute teacher:

   "Good morning, and welcome to our class. I am the 'Substitute Spokesperson.' I will help you with our class today."

2. Show the "Spokesperson" where the materials the substitute will need are located. Materials may include the lunch folder, work folder, class schedule, teacher's manuals, worksheets, attendance sheets, and extra writing paper and pencils.

3. Model for the "Spokesperson" how to explain some of the classroom routines to the substitute, such as the lunch and bus routines. Have the "Spokesperson" practice explaining the routines.

4. If you are designating other students for helping the substitute with specific tasks or subjects, review and practice the jobs with them.

Training the Class

1. Inform the students that a substitute will be teaching their class on (day) and that you want the class to work together to help the substitute throughout the day.

2. Explain that they will help the substitute teach more effectively if they follow the behaviors and routines you've taught them.

3. Review the "Teacher Pleaser" list with the class.

4. Explain that you will ask the substitute to rate the class, at the end of the day, on how well they did with each of the behaviors.

5. Show the students how the substitute will rate the students, telling them what the different scores mean.

6. Explain that then the class will earn additional free time, a class game, a movie, or an extra recess when you return if the substitute has scored each of their behaviors at a 3 or above. However, if the substitute has rated any items below a score of 3, the class will have to practice the behavior(s) during recess when you return.

7. Show the behaviors to the students. Have them practice using them.

8. Rate the students during part of a day or a whole day before the substitute arrives using the rating sheet.

9. At the end of the day, tell the students their scores and discuss any items with a score below 3. Set a time for the students to practice those behaviors during nonacademic time.

Behaving for Substitute Teachers:
Getting students to stick to the program.

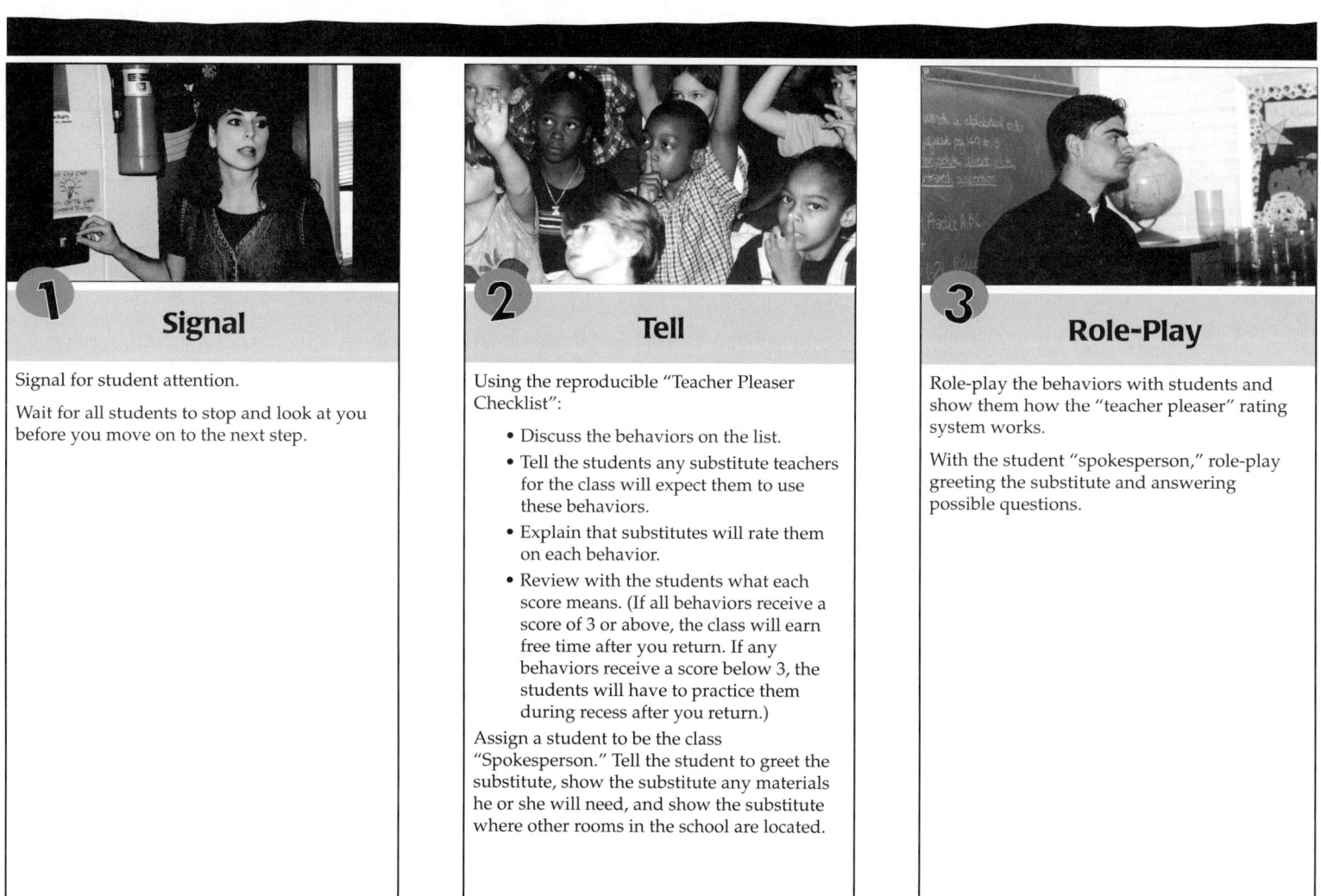

1 Signal

Signal for student attention.

Wait for all students to stop and look at you before you move on to the next step.

2 Tell

Using the reproducible "Teacher Pleaser Checklist":

- Discuss the behaviors on the list.
- Tell the students any substitute teachers for the class will expect them to use these behaviors.
- Explain that substitutes will rate them on each behavior.
- Review with the students what each score means. (If all behaviors receive a score of 3 or above, the class will earn free time after you return. If any behaviors receive a score below 3, the students will have to practice them during recess after you return.)

Assign a student to be the class "Spokesperson." Tell the student to greet the substitute, show the substitute any materials he or she will need, and show the substitute where other rooms in the school are located.

3 Role-Play

Role-play the behaviors with students and show them how the "teacher pleaser" rating system works.

With the student "spokesperson," role-play greeting the substitute and answering possible questions.

4 Monitor

For one day or for several classes before the substitute arrives, rate student behavior on a practice checklist.

Praise students if you rate all items at or above a score of 3. Provide free time or another reward.

If you rate any item below a score of 3, reteach the steps for that routine and set a time for students to practice during recess, after school, or at another free time.

5 Prepare Materials for Substitute

Prepare the following materials for the substitute:

- A folder containing drill activities
- Lesson plans
- A seating chart
- A Teacher Please Checklist

Tell the student "Spokesperson" where these materials will be located in the classroom.

6 Feedback from Substitute

After you return to school, examine the Teacher Pleaser Checklist.

Report the scores to the students.

If all behaviors received a score of 3 or above, praise the students. Give them free time or an activity that you promised them on the day you return.

If any behaviors received a score below 3, reteach the steps and have the students practice during recess, free time, or after school on the day that you return.

Reproducibles

Absent Assignment Reproducible 1

Name: _____   **Absent Partner:** _____

Date: _____

①

Subject: _____

We read pages _____ **in the book** _____

During seatwork, we worked on: _____

The worksheets we worked on were: _____

The homework we need to do is: _____

②

Subject: _____

We read pages _____ **in the book** _____

During seatwork, we worked on: _____

The worksheets we worked on were: _____

The homework we need to do is: _____

③

Subject: _____

We read pages _____ **in the book** _____

During seatwork, we worked on: _____

The worksheets we worked on were: _____

The homework we need to do is: _____

④

Other things you need to know: _____

Absent Assignment Reproducible 2

Student's Name: _____ Partner's Name: _____ Date: _____

1 Subject: _____

    IN CLASS   Checked by Teacher

        What we read: _____ _____

        What we completed for seatwork:_____ _____

        What we completed in groups: _____ _____

        Worksheets we worked on: _____ _____

        Other things you need to know: _____ _____

    FOR HOMEWORK

        What we need to do: _____ _____

        Other things you need to know: _____ _____

2 Subject: _____

    IN CLASS   Checked by Teacher

        What we read: _____ _____

        What we completed for seatwork:_____ _____

        What we completed in groups: _____ _____

        Worksheets we worked on: _____ _____

        Other things you need to know: _____ _____

    FOR HOMEWORK

        What we need to do: _____ _____

        Other things you need to know: _____ _____

3 Subject: _____

    IN CLASS   Checked by Teacher

        What we read: _____ _____

        What we completed for seatwork:_____ _____

        What we completed in groups: _____ _____

        Worksheets we worked on: _____ _____

        Other things you need to know: _____ _____

    FOR HOMEWORK

        What we need to do: _____ _____

        Other things you need to know: _____ _____

Teacher Pleaser Checklist

Substitute Teacher: _____ **Date:** _____

My class has been instructed on how to behave with a substitute teacher. I would appreciate information on their behavior. The following checklist covers behaviors the class has been taught to use. At the end of the day, please rate how well the class did with each of these behaviors so I can help the students continue to improve in these areas. Please be honest. I need to know which behaviors the class does well and which behaviors they need to practice.

To complete the checklist, please circle the number for each item that best describes the overall behavior of the class today. The class has been told that they will earn free time if all of their scores are 3 or above when I return.

Teacher Pleasers	Everyone did a great job	Class did a good job	Class was able to do this sometimes	Class could use more practice	Class was unable to do this correctly
1 Raised hand for help and waited quietly until you could provide assistance	5	4	3	2	1
2 Answered questions or spoke out loud only after being called on	5	4	3	2	1
3 Looked at you and listened quietly when you gave directions	5	4	3	2	1
4 Stayed in seat unless they were given permission to get up	5	4	3	2	1
5 Followed directions quickly	5	4	3	2	1
6 Prepared quickly for each subject	5	4	3	2	1
7 Completed work quietly	5	4	3	2	1
8 Worked on puzzle quietly when they completed their work	5	4	3	2	1
9 Spoke politely to you	5	4	3	2	1
10 Walked, did not run, in the classroom and other school areas	5	4	3	2	1
11 Walked in line quietly	5	4	3	2	1

Please list any students who were difficult and tell me what they did.

Student	Behaviors	Comments

Would you be willing to substitute for this class in the future? _____

Please provide any other feedback on the back of this form.

Substitute Class Schedule and Lesson Plan

Helper	Time	Teacher will:	Students will:

Classroom Checklists

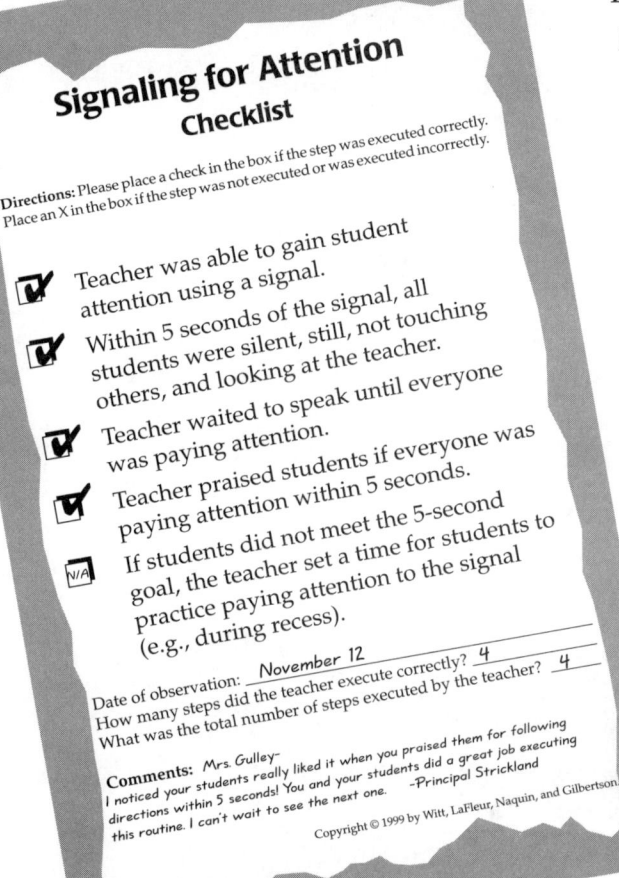

Signaling for Attention
Checklist

Directions: Please place a check in the box if the step was executed correctly. Place an X in the box if the step was not executed or was executed incorrectly.

☑ Teacher was able to gain student attention using a signal.

☑ Within 5 seconds of the signal, all students were silent, still, not touching others, and looking at the teacher.

☑ Teacher waited to speak until everyone was paying attention.

☑ Teacher praised students if everyone was paying attention within 5 seconds.

N/A If students did not meet the 5-second goal, the teacher set a time for students to practice paying attention to the signal (e.g., during recess).

Date of observation: _November 12_
How many steps did the teacher execute correctly? _4_
What was the total number of steps executed by the teacher? _4_

Comments: *Mrs. Gulley—*
I noticed your students really liked it when you praised them for following directions within 5 seconds! You and your students did a great job executing this routine. I can't wait to see the next one. —Principal Strickland

Copyright © 1999 by Witt, LaFleur, Naquin, and Gilbertson.

A checklist is provided here to accompany each routine in this book. Each checklist contains the steps of the routine in sequence and multiple lines for checking the steps observed. The recommended procedure is to learn a routine, teach students how to perform the routine, have the students practice the routine until they are proficient at it, and then ask a colleague, supervisor, or the principal to watch the routine in action. The checklist is a way for you to receive feedback about how you executed the routine. The person watching you is to fill in the checklist as the steps occur and then give you feedback about how you did as soon as possible following the routine. The feedback should be specific and focus on the checklist. We recommend that you have someone monitor your teaching of the routine until you are able to execute all the steps correctly and within the allotted time. A different checklist would be used each time. At left is an example of a completed checklist.

Greeting Students as They Arrive at School

Checklist

Directions: Please place a check in the box if the step was executed correctly. Place an X in the box if the step was not executed or was executed incorrectly.

☐ Students remained on the bus until the "Bus Greeter" arrived at the door.

☐ "Bus Greeter" instructed students to walk to their assigned area.

☐ Students *walked* off the bus in single file.

☐ Students walked to their assigned areas.

☐ The "Bus Greeter" redirected students who ran or who did not walk off the bus in single file.

☐ After all students were off the bus, the "Bus Greeter" supervised practice for students who behaved inappropriately.

Date of observation: _____

How many steps did the teacher execute correctly? _____

What was the total number of steps executed by the teacher? _____

Comments:

Greeting Students as They Depart From School

Checklist

Directions: Please place a check in the box if the step was executed correctly. Place an X in the box if the step was not executed or was executed incorrectly.

☐ Teacher announced that the bus numbers were about to be announced over the school intercom.

☐ Teacher reminded students to walk quietly to their bus when their bus number is called.

☐ Teacher stood at classroom door to monitor students in classroom and students in the hallway.

☐ Teacher made sure students sat quietly at their desks until their bus numbers were called and then walked out of the classroom and down the hall.

☐ Staff positioned throughout school made sure students walked (didn't run) to their buses, lined up outside their buses, and walked onto the bus in single file without bothering anybody.

☐ Staff praised students for walking appropriately to and onto their buses.

☐ If a student did not follow directions, the staff member sent the student to the back of the bus line to practice correct bus behavior.

Date of observation: _____

How many steps did the teacher execute correctly? _____

What was the total number of steps executed by the teacher? _____

Comments:

Signaling for Attention
Checklist

Directions: Please place a check in the box if the step was executed correctly. Place an X in the box if the step was not executed or was executed incorrectly.

☐ Teacher was able to gain student attention using a signal.

☐ Within 5 seconds of the signal, all students were silent, still, not touching others, and looking at the teacher.

☐ Teacher waited to speak until everyone was paying attention.

☐ Teacher praised students if everyone was paying attention within 5 seconds.

☐ If students did not meet the 5-second goal, the teacher set a time for students to practice paying attention to the signal (e.g., during recess).

Date of observation: _____

How many steps did the teacher execute correctly? _____

What was the total number of steps executed by the teacher? _____

Comments:

Giving Directions
Checklist

Directions: Please place a check in the box if the step was executed correctly. Place an X in the box if the step was not executed or was executed incorrectly.

☐ Teacher was able to gain student attention using a signal.

☐ Teacher told students what he or she wanted the students to do.

☐ The directions given were specific and clear.

☐ The directions were given one step or statement at a time.

☐ Teacher demonstrated the steps for the students if they were learning the steps for the first time.

☐ Teacher gave signal for students to perform the steps.

☐ Students performed each of the steps.

☐ Teacher monitored each step by scanning the classroom and walking around it.

☐ When necessary, teacher prompted students about correct behavior.

☐ After each step, teacher told students if they had done the step correctly or incorrectly and explained why the missed steps are important.

☐ Students practiced any steps they did incorrectly.

Date of observation: _____

How many steps did the teacher execute correctly? _____

What was the total number of steps executed by the teacher? _____

Comments:

Providing Feedback
Checklist

Directions: Please place a check in the box if the step was executed correctly. Place an X in the box if the step was not executed or was executed incorrectly.

☐ When providing feedback to an individual student, teacher looked directly at the student.

☐ Teacher stood near the student and turned his or her body in the direction of the student.

☐ Teacher clearly described the expected behavior.

☐ Teacher praised the student's work and/or behavior if the student was following directions.

☐ If the student was not following directions appropriately, the teacher told the student the correct behavior to use.

☐ Teacher asked the student if he or she understood the directions.

☐ Teacher checked back with the student to see if the student was using the correct behavior.

Date of observation: _____

How many steps did the teacher execute correctly? _____

What was the total number of steps executed by the teacher? _____

Comments:

Providing Correction
Checklist

Directions: Please place a check in the box if the step was executed correctly. Place an X in the box if the step was not executed or was executed incorrectly.

☐ Teacher noticed misbehavior and signaled student to stop.

☐ Teacher reminded the student about the correct rule or procedure.

☐ Teacher provided a rationale for the rule or procedure.

☐ Teacher provided overcorrection. That is, the student was directed to perform a task that would compensate for the misbehavior above and beyond its actual ramification.

☐ If possible, teacher had the student overcorrect the misbehavior immediately. If that was not possible, teacher set a time for student to fix the situation during nonacademic time.

☐ Teacher monitored the student completing the task and redirected the student when necessary.

☐ After the student completed the work, teacher provided feedback by reviewing the rule that was broken with the student and giving an expectation for behavior from now on.

Date of observation: _____

How many steps did the teacher execute correctly? _____

What was the total number of steps executed by the teacher? _____

Comments:

Complying With Teacher's Directions
Checklist

Directions: Please place a check in the box if the step was executed correctly. Place an X in the box if the step was not executed or was executed incorrectly.

☐ Teacher was able to gain student attention using a signal.

☐ Teacher gave clear directions to the students in the form of a statement, not a question.

☐ Teacher monitored the students for compliance with the directions given.

☐ If the students complied within 10 seconds, the teacher praised them.

☐ If a student *did not* comply, the teacher gave a warning:

"_____, I need you to _____ now."
   (Name)   (task)

☐ If the student complied, after the warning, the teacher praised the student for complying quickly.

☐ If the student *did not* comply, after the warning, the teacher told the student what he or she would need to practice and when:

"_____, it seems you do not understand how to follow directions. You will need to stay in at the next recess to practice with me."

☐ Teacher applied additional consequences if the student continued to disrupt the class or be disrespectful.

Date of observation: _____

How many steps did the teacher execute correctly? _____

What was the total number of steps executed by the teacher? _____

Comments:

Grading on the Spot
Checklist

Directions: Please place a check in the box if the step was executed correctly. Place an X in the box if the step was not executed or was executed incorrectly.

☐ Teacher wrote step-by-step directions on the board for the work the students were to do and provided examples for the students to follow.

☐ Teacher walked around the room to monitor students' work throughout the working session.

☐ Teacher circled any incorrect answers and wrote his or her initials after the last problem checked whenever she looked at students' work.

☐ One-on-one with the students, teacher retaught any missed steps.

☐ At the end of the working session, teacher provided general feedback to individual students and the class about their progress.

☐ Teacher collected the papers, reviewed students' corrections to problems that had been marked wrong, and checked the problems not checked previously.

Date of observation: _____

How many steps did the teacher execute correctly? _____

What was the total number of steps executed by the teacher? _____

Comments:

Requesting Assistance
Checklist

Directions: Please place a check in the box if the step was executed correctly. Place an X in the box if the step was not executed or was executed incorrectly.

❑ Teacher scanned the room during work time for the student signal for help (i.e., the signal the teacher taught the students to use to request his or her assistance).

❑ Teacher walked up to any student signaling for help and asked what the student needed.

❑ Teacher provided assistance when request was appropriate.

❑ Teacher redirected any students who did not request help in the appropriate manner.
"You are not asking for help in the correct way. You need to _____. Go back to work. In 2 minutes, you may ask for help again."

❑ After giving such redirection, teacher watched for the student's correct use of the signal.

❑ If the student asked for help inappropriately a second time, teacher assisted the student but set a time for the student to practice during a free period.

Date of observation: _____

How many steps did the teacher execute correctly? _____

What was the total number of steps executed by the teacher? _____

Comments:

Beginning the School Day
Checklist

Directions: Please place a check in the box if the step was executed correctly. Place an X in the box if the step was not executed or was executed incorrectly.

❑ Teacher posted the daily assignment for students on the board or overhead before school began.

❑ Teacher was present at the student line-up area before the morning bell rang to monitor their line-up behavior.

❑ Teacher signaled for student attention 10–15 seconds before the morning bell rang.

❑ Teacher told students what they should do (e.g., "When you get into class, I need you to begin working on the daily assignment. You are to begin working within 5 minutes.").

❑ Teacher admitted the students into the classroom only after they were quiet and in line.

❑ Teacher monitored student compliance by scanning and walking around the room.

❑ Teacher praised the students if they followed his or her directions.

❑ Teacher corrected students or repeated the routine if students did not follow the directions.

❑ Teacher completed administrative duties as students worked on the assignment.

Date of observation: _____

How many steps did the teacher execute correctly? _____

What was the total number of steps executed by the teacher? _____

Comments:

Sharpening Pencils
Checklist

Directions: Please place a check in the box if the step was executed correctly. Place an X in the box if the step was not executed or was executed incorrectly.

☐ Teacher gained student attention.

☐ Teacher told students to place their dull pencils on the upper right-hand corner of their desk.

☐ Teacher reminded the student designated as the "Pencil Captain" to collect the dull pencils and replace them with sharpened ones when he or she gives the signal.

☐ Teacher monitored students placing their dull or broken pencils on their desk.

☐ Teacher signaled the "Pencil Captain" to collect the dull pencils and replace them with sharpened ones.

☐ Teacher reminded students to use their extra pencil during the day when needed and to raise their hand for permission to get a new pencil if both pencils are broken or become too dull.

☐ Teacher praised students for exchanging pencils appropriately.

☐ If students did not follow the directions, the teacher set a time for them to practice exchanging pencils during free time or recess.

Date of observation: _____

How many steps did the teacher execute correctly? _____

What was the total number of steps executed by the teacher? _____

Comments:

Ending the School Day
Checklist

Directions: Please place a check in the box if the step was executed correctly. Place an X in the box if the step was not executed or was executed incorrectly.

☐ Teacher posted the homework assignments and a list of the materials the students would need to bring home in a place that was visible to all students.

☐ The "Homework Captain" signaled the teacher 10 minutes before the end-of-school bell.

☐ Teacher went over the assignments and materials with the students and reminded them to write their assignments in their homework notebook, take out the materials to go home, and place their notebook on the corner of their desks.

☐ Teacher told the students to clean their desk area and assigned classroom area, if any.

☐ Teacher monitored for compliance and redirected students when needed.

☐ The "Homework Captain" walked to each desk to check the notebooks. The captain put a check by the names of the students who wrote their homework assignments correctly in a class roster the teacher provided.

☐ If students followed directions, the teacher praised them.

☐ If students did not follow directions, the teacher set a time to practice.

☐ If there was time left over, the teacher reviewed the day's lessons with an activity.

Date of observation: _____

How many steps did the teacher execute correctly? _____

What was the total number of steps executed by the teacher? _____

Comments:

Independent Practice
Checklist

Directions: Please place a check in the box if the step was executed correctly. Place an X in the box if the step was not executed or was executed incorrectly.

☐ Before assigning independent seatwork, teacher checked for student understanding of the skill to be practiced by having students answer questions.

☐ Teacher stated and modeled what the students were to do.

☐ Teacher broke down the directions into small steps for the students to follow.

☐ Teacher practiced several problems with the students.

☐ Teacher wrote the assigned problems and/or page numbers clearly in a visible location.

☐ Teacher reminded students about the rules to follow when working independently (e.g., stay in seat, keep eyes on paper).

☐ Teacher told students how long they had to complete the work, set a timer, and said "Begin."

☐ Teacher monitored students working and the accuracy of their work by walking around the room.

☐ When helping students, teacher positioned him- or herself in a way that would allow continued monitoring of class behavior.

☐ Teacher redirected students who were off task.

☐ After the timer rang, teacher praised students on their work and behavior if they followed directions.

☐ Teacher gave extra work to students whose behavior was off task or instructed them to practice independent seatwork during free time.

☐ Teacher collected student papers or had the students grade them.

Date of observation: _____

How many steps did the teacher execute correctly? _____

What was the total number of steps executed by the teacher? _____

Comments:

Copyright © 1999 by Witt, LaFleur, Naquin, and Gilbertson.

Student Grading
Checklist

Directions: Please place a check in the box if the step was executed correctly. Place an X in the box if the step was not executed or was executed incorrectly.

☐ Teacher instructed students to clear off their desks except for red pens and the papers to be graded.

☐ If students exchanged papers for grading, teacher told them to write their name at the bottom of the paper they would be grading.

☐ Answers were provided in some manner (e.g., teacher or appointed student calling them out or posting them on an overhead).

☐ Students raised their hand quietly if they did not hear or understand answers.

☐ Teacher monitored for raised hands and responded by repeating or explaining answers.

☐ Students marked a "C" if answer was correct and circled any incorrect answers.

☐ Students recorded the number of correct answers at the top of the paper.

☐ Teacher provided students with the opportunity to see their papers and write down any concerns they had.

☐ Teacher randomly reviewed at least two papers to see if they were graded correctly.

☐ If the papers were graded correctly, teacher provided the graders with positive feedback (e.g., praise or a sticker).

☐ If any of the papers were not graded correctly, teacher arranged to meet with the student to review the grading routine during free time.

Date of observation: _____

How many steps did the teacher execute correctly? _____

What was the total number of steps executed by the teacher? _____

Comments:

Copyright © 1999 by Witt, LaFleur, Naquin, and Gilbertson.

Passing In Papers
Checklist

Directions: Please place a check in the box if the step was executed correctly. Place an X in the box if the step was not executed or was executed incorrectly.

☐ Teacher was able to gain student attention using a signal.

☐ Teacher reminded students to write their heading on their papers.

☐ Teacher reminded students of the procedure for passing in papers.

☐ Teacher told the students a time limit, set the timer, and told them to begin.

☐ Teacher scanned the room to see whether students were following the procedure correctly and walked around the room to spot-check the headings.

☐ Teacher picked up papers he or she saw that had improper headings and set a time with the student(s) to practice.

☐ Teacher prompted the "Paper Captain" to pick up the papers and place them in a work-completed file.

☐ Papers were passed in and collected within 2 minutes after teacher directions.

☐ Teacher praised students if they followed directions.

☐ If students did not follow direction, teacher corrected them and repeated the routine or set a time for the students to practice during a free period.

Date of observation: _____

How many steps did the teacher execute correctly? _____

What was the total number of steps executed by the teacher? _____

Comments:

Putting Everything in Its Place
Checklist

Directions: Please place a check in the box if the step was executed correctly. Place an X in the box if the step was not executed or was executed incorrectly.

☐ Teacher was able to gain student attention using a signal.

☐ Teacher told students what needs to be cleaned.

☐ Teacher reminded students of the rules for cleaning.

☐ Teacher told students the amount of time they would have.

☐ Teacher walked around the room to monitor cleaning.

☐ Students walked and talked quietly while cleaning.

☐ After they were done cleaning, students returned to their desks, sat, and waited quietly.

☐ Teacher praised the students if cleaning was done well and completed within the time limit.

☐ If an area was not cleaned well, the teacher told students how the area should look and where materials should be.

☐ If cleaning was not completed within the time limit, the teacher set a time for students to complete the job (immediately or during recess).

☐ In the latter two cases, teacher set a time for students to practice cleaning their area correctly and within the time limit.

Date of observation: _____

How many steps did the teacher execute correctly? _____

What was the total number of steps executed by the teacher? _____

Comments:

Making Up Missed Work
Checklist

Directions: Please place a check in the box if the step was executed correctly. Place an X in the box if the step was not executed or was executed incorrectly.

☐ When taking attendance, teacher reminded the partners of absent students to pick up an Absent Assignment Form for their partner.

☐ Teacher reminded the partners to keep forms on the corner of their desks and fill them out as each subject is taught.

☐ Teacher periodically monitored Absent Assignment Forms during the day to be sure they were complete.

☐ Teacher provided time at the end of the day for the partners to complete the form and gather the work materials the absent student would need.

☐ Teacher directed the partners to take the work materials and Absent Assignment Form to the designated location at the end of the day.

☐ If the partners completed the form accurately and gathered all the necessary materials, the teacher praised them.

☐ If a partner did not complete the form accurately or did not gather all the necessary materials, the teacher set a time to meet with him or her during recess or free time to reteach and practice the routine.

Date of observation: _____

How many steps did the teacher execute correctly? _____

What was the total number of steps executed by the teacher? _____

Comments:

Transitioning
Checklist

Directions: Please place a check in the box if the step was executed correctly. Place an X in the box if the step was not executed or was executed incorrectly.

☐ Teacher was able to gain student attention using a signal.

☐ Teacher told the students specifically what they need to do regarding both academics and behavior.

☐ Teacher gave the students a time limit for completing the steps.

☐ Teacher provided an opportunity to practice if the task was complex.

☐ Teacher scanned the room for student compliance.

☐ Teacher walked around the room prompting students who were off task.

☐ Teacher praised students if they followed the directions correctly and completed the steps within the time limit.

☐ If any students did not follow the directions correctly or did not complete the steps within the time limit, the teacher arranged for them to practice the transition steps during free time or recess.

☐ Students began the next activity within 4 minutes.

Date of observation: _____
How many steps did the teacher execute correctly? _____
What was the total number of steps executed by the teacher? _____

Comments:

Breaking Into Small Learning Groups
Checklist

Directions: Please place a check in the box if the step was executed correctly. Place an X in the box if the step was not executed or was executed incorrectly.

❐ Teacher gained student attention using a signal.

❐ Teacher told the students they would be breaking into small groups and told them where the groups would be located.

❐ Teacher told the students which materials they would need to bring to their groups.

❐ Teacher told the students the activity to be completed.

❐ Teacher reminded the students to walk quietly to their group when their name or row is called.

❐ Teacher told the students a time limit for getting into their groups and ready for the activity.

❐ Teacher walked around the room to monitor student progress.

❐ Teacher praised students if they followed the directions correctly and completed the steps of the routine within the time limit.

❐ If any students did not follow the directions correctly or did not complete the steps within the time limit, the teacher arranged for them to practice breaking into groups during a free period or recess.

Date of observation: _____

How many steps did the teacher execute correctly? _____

What was the total number of steps executed by the teacher? _____

Comments:

Copyright © 1999 by Witt, LaFleur, Naquin, and Gilbertson.

Taking a Bathroom Break
Checklist

Directions: Please place a check in the box if the step was executed correctly. Place an X in the box if the step was not executed or was executed incorrectly.

❐ A Bathroom Notebook was used for students to sign out and in when they needed to use the bathroom during class time.

❐ Students walked to the notebook quietly and without bothering anybody, signed out, and left the room quietly.

❐ Students reentered the classroom quietly, wrote the time they returned in the notebook, and walked quietly to their working areas.

❐ The "Bathroom Captain" checked the time written in the book.

❐ Teacher redirected any students who did not walk or sign out of the classroom following the bathroom break rules and arranged a time for the student to practice during recess or a free period.

❐ Teacher provided praise to students who used the bathroom privilege appropriately.

Date of observation: _____

How many steps did the teacher execute correctly? _____

What was the total number of steps executed by the teacher? _____

Comments:

Copyright © 1999 by Witt, LaFleur, Naquin, and Gilbertson.

Lining Up and Walking
Checklist

Directions: Please place a check in the box if the step was executed correctly. Place an X in the box if the step was not executed or was executed incorrectly.

☐ Teacher gained student attention using a signal.

☐ Teacher told students the destination they'd be walking to and the materials they'd need to take with them.

☐ Teacher gave directions to the location, if necessary.

☐ Teacher told the students to walk slowly to the line as their names or groups were called, with no talking and keeping their hands to themselves.

☐ Teacher told students a time limit for lining up.

☐ Teacher directed students to the line.

☐ Teacher monitored students' progress by scanning and walking around the room.

☐ Teacher redirected students as necessary.

☐ Students were lined up within 4 minutes.

☐ When outside the classroom, teacher positioned him- or herself to be able to monitor all students at all times.

☐ Teacher praised students if they followed the directions correctly.

☐ Teacher arranged a time for students to practice if they did not follow the directions correctly.

Date of observation: _____

How many steps did the teacher execute correctly? _____

What was the total number of steps executed by the teacher? _____

Comments:

Getting Ready for and Returning From Recess
Checklist

Directions: Please place a check in the box if the step was executed correctly. Place an X in the box if the step was not executed or was executed incorrectly.

☐ Teacher signaled for student attention approximately 2 minutes before recess.

☐ Teacher told the students how to prepare for recess (e.g., exchanging dull pencils for sharp ones and clearing off their desks).

☐ Teacher passed out worksheets or assigned an activity for students to begin after recess.

☐ Teacher monitored students' progress in preparing for recess by scanning and walking around the room.

☐ Teacher prompted or redirected students who were not preparing for recess.

☐ Teacher excused students for recess after their working materials were prepared as directed and they were quiet.

☐ At the end of recess and before the students entered the room, the teacher reminded them that they would have 1 minute to walk to their desks and begin their work.

☐ Teacher monitored students' progress by scanning and walking around the room.

☐ Teacher prompted students to work if needed.

☐ Students were working in their seats within 1 minute.

☐ Teacher praised students if they followed the directions correctly.

☐ Teacher arranged a time for students to practice if they did not follow the directions correctly.

☐ Teacher prepared for the next activity, handled student problems, or checked previous work as the students worked on the after-recess activity.

Date of observation: _____

How many steps did the teacher execute correctly? _____

What was the total number of steps executed by the teacher? _____

Comments:

Welcoming Visitors
Checklist

Directions: Please place a check in the box if the step was executed correctly. Place an X in the box if the step was not executed or was executed incorrectly.

☐ Teacher continued teaching when an unannounced visitor entered the classroom.

☐ The "Student Ambassador" greeted the visitor, showed the visitor where to sit, and gave the visitor the Greeting Letter.

☐ Teacher prompted the "Ambassador" to greet the visitor if he or she did not do so within 10 seconds.

☐ Teacher continued the lesson until reaching a good stopping point.

☐ Teacher assigned independent seatwork for students to work on while he or she met with the visitor.

☐ Teacher told the students to work quietly.

☐ Teacher praised the "Ambassador" and the class if the directions were followed.

☐ Teacher reminded the "Ambassador" of steps missed if needed.

☐ Teacher provided a time for the class to practice quietly working on independent seatwork if needed.

Date of observation: _____

How many steps did the teacher execute correctly? _____

What was the total number of steps executed by the teacher? _____

Comments:

Free Time Behavior
Checklist

Directions: Please place a check in the box if the step was executed correctly. Place an X in the box if the step was not executed or was executed incorrectly.

☐ Teacher organized materials and the locations for activities.

☐ Teacher gained student attention using a signal.

☐ Teacher told the students why they were being given free time and how much time they would have.

☐ Teacher told the students the activities they could choose from, how to do the activities, where to do the activities, and how to talk during the activities.

☐ Teacher set a timer.

☐ Teacher scanned students as they worked.

☐ Teacher redirected students who were not participating in an appropriate activity.

☐ When the timer went off, teacher signaled and monitored for student attention.

☐ Teacher provided cleaning directions.

☐ Teacher praised students if, after free time, everything was clean and in its place.

☐ Teacher arranged a time for students to practice if the classroom was not cleaned correctly.

Date of observation: _____

How many steps did the teacher execute correctly? _____

What was the total number of steps executed by the teacher? _____

Comments:

Lunchroom Behavior
Checklist

Directions: Please place a check in the box if the step was executed correctly. Place an X in the box if the step was not executed or was executed incorrectly.

❒ Two minutes prior to lunchtime, teacher gained student attention using a signal.

❒ Teacher reviewed appropriate lunchroom behavior.

❒ Teacher told the students to retrieve their lunches or lunch money and line up quietly.

❒ The class lined up quietly and walked to the lunchroom.

❒ Teacher monitored lunchroom behavior by visually scanning and walking around the tables.

❒ Teacher redirected students who were out of their seats, talking loudly, playing with their food, or running in the halls or cafeteria.

❒ One minute before the end of lunch period, teacher signaled for student attention.

❒ Teacher scanned to see if the tables were clean except for the students' trays. If any tables were not clean, teacher directed students to clean the tables within 1 minute.

❒ Students returned trays, recycled supplies, and threw out trash quietly.

❒ Teacher redirected students who did not follow the directions.

❒ Teacher praised students who were compliant.

❒ Students lined up quietly and walked back to the classroom.

Date of observation: _____

How many steps did the teacher execute correctly? _____

What was the total number of steps executed by the teacher? _____

Comments:

Behaving for Substitute Teachers
Checklist

Directions: Please place a check in the box if the step was executed correctly. Place an X in the box if the step was not executed or was executed incorrectly.

❒ Teacher gained student attention using a signal.

❒ Teacher told the students the behaviors that any substitute teacher would expect the class to use, that the substitute would rate their behavior, what the rating scores mean, and how the students could earn a reward for following the Teacher Pleaser behaviors.

❒ Teacher assigned and trained a "Spokesperson" to help the substitute with schedules, materials, and locating other rooms around the school.

❒ Teacher role-played the behaviors with the students and showed them how the rating system works.

❒ Students practiced the behaviors while the teacher monitored and rated the students using the checklist.

❒ On the day the teacher was absent, the student "Spokesperson" greeted the substitute and showed him or her around the classroom and school.

❒ The substitute had been given a folder containing drill activities, lesson plans, a seating chart, and the Teacher Pleaser Checklist.

❒ When the teacher returned, he or she praised the students if the substitute rated all behaviors with a score of 3 or above and provided a positive consequence, such as free time.

❒ If any behavior received a score below 3, the teacher retaught the behavior and set a time for students to practice it during a free period.

Date of observation: _____

How many steps did the teacher execute correctly? _____

What was the total number of steps executed by the teacher? _____

Comments:

Student
Training Overheads

Teaching students how to accomplish and become proficient with classroom routines may require a variety of teaching strategies. One strategy is to teach from an overhead, which is a visual of what is to be learned.

In this section, an overhead transparency master is provided for each routine. As you begin to teach a routine, we recommend showing the transparency and going over each step of the routine. If you are using the teaching model TELL, SHOW, DO, during the TELL part you would refer to the transparency and tell the students each behavior involved in each step of the routine. After students learn the steps, you can review them by covering up all but the first step on the transparency and asking the students to tell you the second step, the third step, and so forth.

If students are having a difficult time learning a routine, make sure that they understand the routine and are able to perform it. Try out the routine yourself before having the students learn it. It might also be a good idea to have a colleague watch you teach the routine and provide feedback. (See the section on Checklists.)

The SHOW part of the transparency gives teaching strategies that can be used to reinforce the steps learned. With these strategies, you actually model what the students are to do. If the students are supposed to notice a signal you give, for example, you could ask a student to come to the front of the room, act as the teacher, and perform the signal. You would then demonstrate how to notice the signal, stop talking, stop what you are doing, and look at the teacher. After you model the steps, you would have individual students and the whole class perform them. You would then provide feedback to the students about how they did on each step. Do not let the students practice the steps incorrectly. For example, if the students did not stop what they were doing after you gave them a signal, have them practice that step until they perform it the right way.

The DO part of the teaching strategy comes into play after the students have correctly modeled all of the steps of a routine. At that point, you would tell the students that it is time to chart how much they know about the routine. Explain that you will be using the chart on the overhead for this purpose. Let them know that this is their chance to show you how much they have learned.

Tell the students that you are going to have them practice the routine exactly as it is to occur, with everyone doing each step correctly. If the routine calls for the students to line up and go to the gym, they would perform all the steps of that routine, ending up at the gym. Explain that on the overhead, you will chart the steps they have done correctly and those they have done incorrectly. For example, if they do steps 1, 2, 4, and 5 correctly but do step 3 incorrectly, you would write "1, 2, 4, 5" in the "Steps Done Correctly" column and "3" in the "Steps Done Incorrectly" column. You would then explain the step(s) they have done wrong, reteach them, and have the students practice some more. With each trial, you would record the results on the chart to give the students a visual record of their progress.

It is important to provide the students with a practice goal. Tell them that you expect them to do the routine correctly within three learning trials. If they do not execute all of the steps accurately and within the time limit given by the third trial, you will have to have them practice again at recess. Of course, it is always best to be positive. Tell the students that you know they will get the routine right the first time—and if not the first time, then the second time for sure!

Whenever students execute all of the steps of a new routine correctly, reinforce their behavior with verbal praise. It may also be appropriate to provide the students with a reinforcing activity, such as give them 2-3 extra minutes for recess or free play. If any students do not execute the steps correctly, have them practice during their recess time. This practice is often most effective when, at the same time the students who did not comply with the directions are practicing, others who did a good job are enjoying extra recess.

Arriving at School

Use with "Escorting Students To and From School" routine.

TELL

1 Remain seated until a "Bus Greeter" comes to the bus door.

2 Walk single file out of the bus without bothering others. Walk to your assigned area.

3 Wait quietly for instructions.

SHOW

1 Teacher models the steps.

2 Student volunteers model the steps.

3 Teacher provides feedback as students model.

DO

Practice Times	Steps Done Correctly	Steps Done Incorrectly
1		
2		
3		

Departing From School

Use with "Greeting and Escorting Students To and From School" routine.

TELL

1. Bus numbers will be announced on the intercom at the end of the day as the buses arrive.

2. Sit quietly at your desk listening for your bus to be called.

3. When your bus is announced walk to the bus without bothering others.

4. When you get to your bus, form a line on the sidewalk outside the bus door. Then walk quietly in single file onto the bus without bothering or touching others.

SHOW

1. Teacher models the steps.

2. Student volunteers model the steps.

3. Teacher provides feedback as students model.

DO

Practice Times	Steps Done Correctly	Steps Done Incorrectly
1		
2		
3		

When the Teacher Signals

TELL

When I give the signal, you have five seconds to:

1. Notice the signal.
2. Be quiet, stop what you are doing, and look at me.
3. Wait for my directions.

SHOW

1. Teacher models the steps.
2. Students volunteers model the steps.
3. Teacher provides feedback as students model.

DO

Practice Times	Steps Done Correctly	Steps Done Incorrectly
1		
2		
3		

Following Directions

Use with "Giving Directions" and "Ensuring Student Compliance" routines.

TELL

1. Notice my signal for attention. Stop what you are doing and look at me.

2. Listen quietly as I tell you what I want you to do.

3. Watch as I show you what I want you to do. If you have a question, raise your hand to get my attention and ask your question when I call your name.

4. Listen for my signal to do the steps.

5. Do exactly what I have told you to do.

6. When you are finished, look at me and wait quietly for more directions.

SHOW

1. Teacher models the steps.

2. Student volunteers model the steps.

3. Teacher provides feedback as students model.

DO

Practice Times	Steps Done Correctly	Steps Done Incorrectly
1		
2		
3		

Accepting Feedback

Use with "Providing Feedback" routine.

TELL

1. Stop what you are doing and look at me when I signal for your attention.

2. Listen as I tell you about your behavior. If the behavior was incorrect, listen quietly to how you can correct the problem.

3. Ask me to explain the behavior if you are not sure how to do it correctly.

4. Return to your activity using the correct behavior.

SHOW

1. Teacher models the steps.

2. Student volunteers model the steps.

3. Teacher provides feedback as students model.

DO

Practice Times	Steps Done Correctly	Steps Done Incorrectly
1		
2		
3		

Accepting Correction

Use with "Providing Correction" routine.

TELL

1. Stop what you are doing and look at me when I signal for your attention.

2. Listen as I tell you about the rule that needs to be followed.

3. Listen as I tell you why the rule is needed.

4. Listen to my directions.

5. Practice the rule in the correct way several times.

6. When you are finished, look at me and wait quietly for more directions.

SHOW

1. Teacher models the steps.

2. Student volunteers model the steps.

3. Teacher provides feedback as students model.

DO

Practice Times	Steps Done Correctly	Steps Done Incorrectly
1		
2		
3		

Ensuring Student Compliance

TELL

1. At my signal, stop what you are doing and quietly look at me.

2. Listen to my directions.

3. Watch how directions need to be completed.

4. Listen for my signal to start following the directions.

5. Follow my directions immediately.

6. You are not following directions if you hear me give a warning such as, "Please, I need you to _____ now or you will be practicing _____ during recess."

7. If you do not follow directions after the warning, you will be told to meet with me to practice complying with my directions during the next recess.

8. You will need to meet me at the beginning of recess.

SHOW

1. Teacher models the steps.

2. Student volunteers model the steps.

3. Teacher provides feedback as students model.

DO

Practice Times	Steps Done Correctly	Steps Done Incorrectly
1		
2		
3		

Grading on the Spot

TELL

1. I will walk around the room, looking at your work.

2. I will circle any problems on your paper that are incorrect.

3. Try to redo all the circled problems. Look at examples on the board or in the book to see how to solve the problems correctly.

4. If you continue to have trouble with a problem, signal for help. Then continue working on the rest of the problems while you wait for assistance.

5. At my signal, pass in your papers.

SHOW

1. Teacher models the steps.

2. Student volunteers model the steps.

3. Teacher provides feedback as students model.

DO

Practice Times	Steps Done Correctly	Steps Done Incorrectly
1		
2		
3		

Requesting Assistance

TELL

1 Use the signal when you need help with your work. Wait quietly for me to respond. As you wait, do other work or read quietly.

2 When I get to your desk, tell me what you are having difficulty with. When I finish helping you, return to work quickly.

3 If you use the signal incorrectly, I will explain what you are doing wrong. You won't receive help until you use the correct signal. If you use the signal incorrectly twice in a row, you will have to practice using the correct signal during free time.

SHOW

1 Teacher models the steps.

2 Student volunteers model the steps.

3 Teacher provides feedback as students model.

DO

Practice Times	Steps Done Correctly	Steps Done Incorrectly
1		
2		
3		

Beginning the School Day

TELL

1. Walk to the morning line-up area. Line up quietly.
2. Notice my signal and look at me quietly.
3. Listen to the directions I give you.
4. Walk into the classroom in an orderly manner when I give you the go-ahead.
5. Listen to any directions I give you.
6. Complete morning work posted in class.
7. Check to make sure you have two sharpened pencils. If you don't, follow the "Sharpening Pencils" routine.
8. Place your homework and any parent notes on the upper right-hand corner of your desk.
9. Begin to work on the daily assignment, which will be on the board or overhead.
10. Continue to work on the assignment until I signal you to stop.

SHOW

1. Teacher models the steps.
2. Student volunteers model the steps.
3. Teacher provides feedback as students model.

DO

Practice Times	Steps Done Correctly	Steps Done Incorrectly
1		
2		
3		

Sharpening Pencils

TELL

1 At (Time of Day), check to see if you have two sharpened pencils.

2 Place your dull or broken pencils on the upper right-hand corner of your desk.

3 The "Pencil Captain" will pick up the dull pencils and replace them with sharpened ones.

4 Use one of the sharpened pencils. Place the other one in your desk.

5 Each day, the "Pencil Captain" will sharpen pencils at (Time of Day).

6 If your pencil breaks during class, use your extra pencil.

SHOW

1 Teacher models the steps.

2 Student volunteers model the steps.

3 Teacher provides feedback as students model.

DO

Practice Times	Steps Done Correctly	Steps Done Incorrectly
1		
2		
3		

Ending the School Day

TELL

1 When the "Homework Captain" signals for my attention, stop what you are doing and look at me.

2 Listen to the directions I give you about your homework and the materials you are to take home.

3 Write your assignments neatly in your homework notebook.

4 Raise your hand to ask questions if you do not understand how to do the homework.

5 After writing down your assignments, leave your homework notebook on the corner of your desk for the "Homework Captain" to check.

6 Then put your notebook and homework materials in your backpack or book bag.

7 Clean your desk area.

8 Clean the classroom area assigned to you.

9 When it is time to go home, take your homework notebook and materials.

SHOW

1 Teacher models the steps.

2 Student volunteers model the steps.

3 Teacher provides feedback as students model.

DO

Practice Times	Steps Done Correctly	Steps Done Incorrectly
1		
2		
3		

Independent Practice

TELL

1. Take an active part in the review session.
2. Listen to my directions.
3. Listen for the time limit I will give you for the independent work.
4. Begin working at my signal.
5. Continue working quietly.
6. Signal for help if you need it.
7. Keep your eyes on your own work.
8. Check your work.
9. Signal when you are finished.
10. If you finish early, do a free time activity.

SHOW

1. Teacher models the steps.
2. Student volunteers model the steps.
3. Teacher provides feedback as students model.

DO

Practice Times	Steps Done Correctly	Steps Done Incorrectly
1		
2		
3		

Student Grading

TELL

1 Clear your desk.

2 Take out a red pen and the paper to be graded.

3 Exchange papers with a partner, if I direct you to do so.

4 Write your name at the bottom of the paper you will grade.

5 Listen for the answers or look at the answers.

6 Signal if you did not hear an answer.

7 Mark a "C" by the correct answers.

8 Circle any incorrect answers.

9 Count the number of correct answers.

10 Write the number of answers that were correct at the top of the paper.

11 If you did not grade your own paper, return the paper you graded to its owner.

12 Look at your grade. With your red pen, circle or write down any concerns you may have about the grading of your work.

13 Pass in your papers when I direct you to without talking or leaving your seat.

SHOW

1 Teacher models the steps.

2 Student volunteers model the steps.

3 Teacher provides feedback as students model.

DO

Practice Times	Steps Done Correctly	Steps Done Incorrectly
1		
2		
3		

Passing In Papers

TELL

1. When I signal you, stop what you are doing and look at me quietly.

2. Look to see if your paper has the proper heading. Be sure it includes: _____
   _____
   _____
   _____

3. Listen to my directions.

4. Quietly wait for the papers in your row to be passed to you. Place yours on top and then quickly and quietly pass the pile to the right.

5. The "Paper Captain" will pick up the papers at the last desk of each row.

6. Wait quietly for directions.

SHOW

1. Teacher models the steps.

2. Student volunteers model the steps.

3. Teacher provides feedback as students model.

DO

Practice Times	Steps Done Correctly	Steps Done Incorrectly
1		
2		
3		

Putting Everything in Its Place

TELL

1. At my signal, stop what you are doing and quietly look at me.
2. Listen to the cleaning directions I give.
3. At my signal, clean your area.
4. Walk and talk quietly while cleaning.
5. Put away all materials neatly.
6. Hand in your completed work.
7. When you are finished, walk to your desk, sit, and wait quietly.

SHOW

1. Teacher models the steps.
2. Student volunteers model the steps.
3. Teacher provides feedback as students model.

DO

Practice Times	Steps Done Correctly	Steps Done Incorrectly
1		
2		
3		

Making Up Missed Work

TELL

1 Notice when your homework partner is absent and pick up an Absent Assignment Form.

2 Fill out the form as each subject is taught.

3 Get an extra copy of any worksheets and any other materials handed out for your partner.

4 Ask me if you do not understand an assignment.

5 At the end of the day, gather together the books and materials your partner will need to complete the work he or she missed and show me what you have collected.

6 Bring the books, materials, and the Absent Assignment Form to the (office, desk, other).

SHOW

1 Teacher models the steps.

2 Student volunteers model the steps.

3 Teacher provides feedback as students model.

DO

Practice Times	Steps Done Correctly	Steps Done Incorrectly
1		
2		
3		

Transitioning

TELL

1 When I give the signal, stop what you are doing and quietly look at me.

2 Listen to the directions I give.

3 Listen for the time limit.

4 When I signal you to start, begin the steps I have explained.

5 Follow the steps quietly and without bothering others. Follow the walking rules. Complete the steps within the time limit.

6 Begin the next activity when I direct you to.

SHOW

1 Teacher models the steps.

2 Student volunteers model the steps.

3 Teacher provides feedback as students model.

DO

Practice Times	Steps Done Correctly	Steps Done Incorrectly
1		
2		
3		

Breaking Into Small Learning Groups

TELL

1. Look and listen for my instructions. I will tell you:
   - Which groups you are to form
   - Where the groups will work
   - Which materials you will need for the activity
   - What the activity will be

2. Use the help signal to ask questions if you don't understand any part of my directions.

3. Gather the materials you will need and quickly and quietly walk to your group when your name or row is called.

4. Sit down and look at me for further direction.

SHOW

1. Teacher models the steps.
2. Student volunteers model the steps.
3. Teacher provides feedback as students model.

DO

Practice Times	Steps Done Correctly	Steps Done Incorrectly
1		
2		
3		

Taking a Bathroom Break

TELL

1 When you exit,

- Walk to the notebook quietly without bothering others.
- Sign your name and write the time in the notebook.
- Walk directly to the bathroom without making noise.
- After using the bathroom, be sure to flush the toilet, wash your hands without splashing, and throw out any trash.

2 When you return,

- Walk directly back to class.
- Write the time that you returned in the notebook.

3 Walk quietly to your desk and listen to directions.

SHOW

1 Teacher models the steps.

2 Student volunteers model the steps.

3 Teacher provides feedback as students model.

DO

Practice Times	Steps Done Correctly	Steps Done Incorrectly
1		
2		
3		

Lining Up and Walking

TELL

1. Notice my signal to line up.
2. Look and listen for my directions.
3. Listen to the time limit.
4. Walk slowly to line.
5. Stand behind the last person in line.
6. Keep your hands and feet to yourself.
7. Remain quiet. There is to be no talking.
8. Stand in line quietly, and listen for directions.

SHOW

1. Teacher models the steps.
2. Student volunteers model the steps.
3. Teacher provides feedback as students model.

DO

Practice Times	Steps Done Correctly	Steps Done Incorrectly
1		
2		
3		

Getting Ready for and Returning From Recess

TELL

Part 1: Getting Ready for Recess

1. Two minutes before recess, I will signal for attention.
2. Stop what you are doing and look at me quietly.
3. Listen to my directions.
4. Clear off your desk.
5. Follow the "Pencil Sharpening" routine.
6. At the same time, I will hand out or make an assignment for you to complete when you return from recess. Place the assignment or the materials you will need on your desk.
7. Wait quietly in the "working student posture" until I excuse you for recess.

Part 2: Returning From Recess

8. When you return from recess, walk quietly into the classroom.
9. Put away your coat and any extra clothing or materials.
10. Walk quietly to your desk, sit down, and listen to my directions.
11. Begin working on the assignment.

SHOW

1. Teacher models the steps.
2. Student volunteers model the steps.
3. Teacher provides feedback as students model.

DO

Practice Times	Steps Done Correctly	Steps Done Incorrectly
1		
2		
3		

Copyright © 1999 by Witt, LaFleur, Naquin, and Gilbertson.

Welcoming Visitors

TELL

The "Ambassador" is in charge of:

1. Keeping the visitor sitting area clean.
2. Greeting the visitor.
3. Inviting the visitor to sit.
4. Giving the visitor the Greeting Letter.
5. Thanking the visitor for being patient.

The rest of the class should do the following when a visitor enters the classroom:

1. Continue working or listening to me.
2. Listen to my directions.
3. Quietly complete the work I assign while I am meeting with the visitor.

SHOW

1. Teacher models the steps.
2. Student volunteers model the steps.
3. Teacher provides feedback as students model.

DO

Practice Times	Steps Done Correctly	Steps Done Incorrectly
1		
2		
3		

Free Time Behavior

TELL

1. At my signal, stop what you are doing and quietly look at me.

2. Listen to my directions.

3. Walk to the activity area and begin the activity.

4. Stay in the area until free time is over.

5. Talk quietly and signal for help if you need it.

6. At my signal, clean your activity area.

7. Walk back to your desk and sit down.

8. Wait quietly for my directions.

SHOW

1. Teacher models the steps.

2. Student volunteers model the steps.

3. Teacher provides feedback as students model.

DO

Practice Times	Steps Done Correctly	Steps Done Incorrectly
1		
2		
3		

Lunchroom Behavior

TELL

① When I signal, stop what you are doing and look at me.

② Walk to get lunch supplies.

③ Line up and wait quietly.

④ At my signal, walk to the lunchroom in an orderly fashion.

⑤ Bring your food to your table or line up in the lunch line, get your food, pay for it, and bring it to your table.

⑥ Remain seated during lunch, and use a quiet voice when talking with your friends.

⑦ Eat your food over the tray. Don't play with your food.

⑧ At my signal, stop what you are doing and look at me.

⑨ Clean your table so that the table is empty when you pick up your trays and walk away.

⑩ Recycle materials, throw away trash, and return your lunch tray and other supplies.

⑪ Line up quietly and wait for my directions.

SHOW

① Teacher models the steps.

② Student volunteers model the steps.

③ Teacher provides feedback as students model.

DO

Practice Times	Steps Done Correctly	Steps Done Incorrectly
①		
②		
③		

Behaving for Substitute Teachers

TELL

The "Substitute Spokesperson" is in charge of:

1. Greeting the substitute.
2. Giving the substitute the Substitute Teacher Folder.
3. Showing the substitute where materials are located.
4. Explaining the class routines to the substitute.
5. Showing the substitute where other rooms in the building are located.

All students are to follow the behaviors on the Teacher Pleaser Checklist:

1. Raise your hand and wait quietly for help.
2. Speak out loud only when you are called on.
3. Listen quietly when you are given directions.
4. Stay in your assigned seat unless you are given permission to get up.
5. Follow directions quickly.
6. Prepare for each subject quickly.
7. Complete your work quietly.
8. Work quietly on the free time activity when you have completed assigned work.
9. Speak politely to the substitute teacher.
10. Walk, don't run, in the classroom and the school.
11. Walk in line quietly.

SHOW

1. Teacher models the steps.
2. Student volunteers model the steps.
3. Teacher provides feedback as students model.

DO

Practice Times	Steps Done Correctly	Steps Done Incorrectly
1		
2		
3		

References

Berliner, D.C. (1989). Effective classroom management and instruction: A knowledge base for consultation. In J.L. Graden, J.E. Zins, & M.J. Curtis (Eds.), *Alternative educational delivery systems: Enhancing instructional options for all students*. Washington, DC: National Association of School Psychologists.

Brophy, J.E. & Good, T. (1986). Teacher behavior and student achievement. In M.C. Wittrock (Ed.), *Handbook of Research on Teaching* (p. 328-375). New York: Macmillan.

Colvin, G., Sugai, G., Good, R.H., & Young-Yon, L. (1997). Using active supervision and precorrection to improve transition behaviors in elementary school. *School Psychology Quarterly, 12*, 344-363.

Emmer, E.T. & Evertson, C.M. (1981). Synthesis of research on classroom management. *Educational Leadership*, 342-347.

Emmer, E.T., Evertson, C.M., & Anderson, L.M. (1980). Effective management at the beginning of the school year. *Elementary School Journal, 80*, 219-231.

Gettinger, M. (1988). Methods of proactive classroom management. *School Psychology Review, 17,* 227-242.

Gilbertson, D.G., Witt, J.C., & LaFleur, L.H. (1997). *Effect of antecedent and consequential strategies to increase teacher implementation of a peer tutoring intervention.* Unpublished manuscript, Louisiana State University, Baton Rouge.

Jenson, W.R., Sloan, H.N., & Young, K.R. (1988). Applied behavior analysis in education: A structured teaching approach (2nd ed.). Englewood Cliffs, NJ: Prentice Hall.

LaFleur, L.H., Witt J.C., Naquin, G., Harwell, V., & Gilbertson, D. (1998). Use of coaching to enhance proactive classroom management by improvement of student transitioning between classroom activities. *Effective School Practices, 17*(2), 70-82.

Rhode, G., Jenson, W.R., & Reavis, H.K. (1992). *The tough kid book: Practical classroom management strategies.* Longmont, CO: Sopris West.

Rosenshine, B. & Stevens, R. (1986). Teaching functions. In M. D. Wittrock (Ed.), *Handbook of research on teaching* (3rd ed.). New York: Macmillan.

Sprick, R. & Howard, L. (1995). *Teacher's encyclopedia of behavior management.* Longmont, CO: Sopris West.

Wurtle, S.K. & Drabman, R.S. (1984). Beat the buzzer for classroom dawdling: A one-year trial. *Behavior Therapy, 15,* 403-409.